Praise for The Author's Toolkit

Reading this felt like sitting down with a wise friend who gets what it means to be an author today. It's honest, strategic, and full of heart. It helps you to stop hiding, show up with confidence, and finally feel seen.

Susan Friedmann, CSP, international bestselling author of *Riches in Niches: How to Make it BIG in a Small Market*

The Author's Toolkit is a magic box of wonders. One by one, the tricks you need as a writer on the edge of publication are unveiled. With the varying styles of the contributing authors, the mystery of a successful book is peeled away, leaving you with concrete steps you can deploy to create your own success. No magic wand required.

KC O'Connell, Writer. Reader. Dreamer.

I'll be keeping *The Author's Toolkit* within arm's reach and recommending it to all my clients. This comprehensive guide shares essential knowledge that every author needs before embarking on their writing journey. It is jam-packed with easily actionable steps and brilliant examples—not just what to do, but when to do it.

Maggie Mills, ghostwriter and writing coach

As someone who works directly with authors, often first-time self-publishing authors, I have no hesitation in recommending *The Author's Toolkit* to my clients and other connections. For those who struggle with marketing, there is plenty of advice that will help authors get the sales their book deserves.

Catherine Williams, founder, Chapter One Book Design

As a marketer with twenty-five years of experience and founder of the Charm City Readers Facebook reading community, *The Author's Toolkit: Mastering the Art of Author Visibility* is a practical and insightful guide to help authors build their brand and connect with readers. Writing a great book is only the beginning. To truly succeed, authors must tell their own stories, be authentic, and create connections. *The Author's Toolkit* provides straightforward yet effective strategies to help authors enhance their book promotion and foster lasting engagement with their audience.

Charissa Costa, founder, Charm City Readers

This book is all you need to support your author's journey, and it's so helpful and easy to read. Keep it on your desk, highlight it, and clip away!

Jennifer McGinley, owner of JLM Strategic Communications

The Author's Toolkit is helping me launch my third book aligned with my authenticity and mission. I have been through this process. With my first book, I had no clue what I was doing with the launch. I was simply thrilled to have a published book, and my husband and I used the "wing and a prayer" method. My second book was a little more systematized, with a gradual build-up to the lunch, but then we fizzled out trying to make anything happen after publication. Our third book comes out in early 2026, and I now know how to organize my social media, bio, and media kit; and we can be a well-organized machine by following the pro tips from *The Author's Toolkit*. I'm giddy and excited to see how many more lives we can impact by having an organized process to promote our work.

Donna Kendrick, CFP®, CDFA®, author of *A Guide for Blended Families* and *A Guide for Widowhood*

The Author's Toolkit is a must-have for all debut authors! It contains everything you need to know as you set out on your promotional journey in an approachable and easily digestible format. I'll be recommending it to all my clients!

Mamie Sanders, founder of MVL Marketing, a boutique digital marketing agency

The Author's Toolkit is clear, thorough, and genuinely supportive. Whether you read it straight through or just flip to the part you need, it gives you exactly what you're looking for and makes the journey feel far less overwhelming.

Kim Keane, Intuitive Healing Coach

THE AUTHOR'S TOOLKIT

THE AUTHOR'S TOOLKIT

Mastering the Art of Author Visibility

CHERI D. ANDREWS, ESQ.   SANDRA BEATTY

HANNE BRØTER   JILL CELESTE, MA

DEBORAH KEVIN, MA   JENNIFER NICHOLS

SUZANNE TREGENZA

HIGHLANDER
PRESS

ISBN: 978-1-956442-58-8
Ebook ISBN: 978-1-956442-59-5
Library of Congress: Applied For.

Published by Highlander Press
501 W. University Pkwy, Ste. B2
Baltimore, MD 21210

Cover design: Hanne Brøter
Managing Editor: Deborah Kevin, MA
Editor: Jill Celeste, MA

To the authors—
who dare to share their truths,
who wrestle with words and still show up on the page,
who believe that stories matter, and
who are brave enough to be seen.

This book is for you.
May your voice be loud, your impact lasting,
and your visibility unmistakable.

The scariest moment is always just before you start.

Stephen King

Contents

Introduction

Deborah Kevin, MA

If there's one thing I know for sure after guiding hundreds of authors through the writing and publishing process, it's this: most writers want to *write*—not market.

And yet, your book's impact doesn't end with "The End." In fact, that's where the real journey begins.

The Author's Toolkit was born out of countless conversations with authors—many of whom had poured their hearts onto the page only to feel lost when it came time to get their book into readers' hands. They'd ask, "Do I need a website?" "How do I get reviews?" "What the heck is an author brand?" (And yes, I've heard every version of that question—including ones with a few extra expletives.)

This toolkit is our answer. It's packed with practical, no-fluff strategies from seasoned experts who know what it takes to be visible as an author today. You'll find chapters on building your brand, writing a bio that doesn't sound like soggy toast (spoiler: that one's mine), crafting your website, leveraging media, and so much more.

But more than that? This book is about helping you show up fully and confidently as *you*. Because readers don't just buy books—they buy connection. They want to know the person behind the pages. Your voice matters. Your story matters. And your presence in the world matters.

So whether you're launching your first book or looking to breathe new life into your author platform, this toolkit will walk beside you step-by-step—offering the same blend of structure, strategy, and encouragement we bring to every Highlander Press project.

Here's to making your message visible. Boldly. Strategically. Authentically.

Deborah Kevin, MA
Founder and Chief Inspiration Officer
Highlander Press

Your Author Foundation

ONE

Author Brand

Hanne Brøter

Think of your favorite author. Now, picture their books. Do you recognize them immediately? That's branding. But here's where most new authors go wrong: They assume their brand is their book cover. It's not.

Your branding is what makes readers recognize you across your entire author career—not just one book at a time. In this chapter, we'll dive into what makes an effective author brand and why it's different from your book's branding.

I am so grateful that this chapter about branding is the first you will read in this book. Because regardless of whether you are a spanking new author or a seasoned one, knowing what branding is and how it can be used, will make things easier for you later. Please keep in mind what you learn in this chapter when you enter later chapters. Your conscious knowledge about branding will influence and inform decisions about your website, your social media presence, your email newsletter, promotional materials, and all your ongoing marketing.

What Is Branding, Exactly?

Branding is something we do in our businesses, organizations, or as persons to differentiate what we do and offer, emphasizing what is unique for our services or, in our case, books. My expertise lies in the visual aspect of branding, and I will focus on this aspect. The purpose of visual branding is differentiation and recognition. You'd want to stand out with your book(s) and want your social media posts, website, email newsletter, and other marketing materials (I call them visual touchpoints) to be swiftly and clearly recognized as yours. You can achieve this by using a consistent "visual language," which is a congruent use of visual means like colors, fonts, imagery, and logos. We gather these for reference in a document, which can be called by various names, including a brand book, a graphic profile, a visual brand guide, and others.

Authors Need Two Visual Branding Profiles

From my experience, I have found that visual branding for authors differs significantly from that of entrepreneurs and businesses. While entrepreneurs have ONE visual branding profile, which includes their overall business and services, authors can be said to have at least TWO, often more!

Let me illustrate this with a few examples: You may develop a visual branding profile for yourself as THE AUTHOR YOU, with a logo (your name), a font, and a branded color palette. BUT should *the cover of every book you eventually will write* be designed within this visual brand scheme? Probably NOT!

A book should be "branded to itself." Does that sound weird? Stay with me, and you'll understand.

The cover is the ONLY illustration allowed for your book, (if you are writing an "ordinary" text-based book.) For this book, the cover is the only place where you can convey something visually. Thus, you want the cover to reflect and enhance the main idea of the book, using photos, illustrations, colors, and fonts that matches the book's content in expression and style. It is not given that your visual author brand will be able to do that. That's why every book should be "branded to its particular content."

Choosing the Proper Profile

A pitfall that follows from the duality of the author/book-branding issue is this: You are a spanking-new author, proudly launching your very first book. It has been designed as an awesome cover where the title and other text are set in a certain font, and certain colors have been used. Now, you are about to create a website! Should you use the colors and fonts from your book cover as the visual branding for your website? I know it is very tempting to do so; the book and the website will match perfectly, and everything will look gorgeous until you publish your second book, a totally different story or topic. This book has demanded a cover *branded to its own particular content*, as we explained above, which WILL NOT match the website because the website was created to match the first book. So, no, unless you plan on writing only one book in your life, do not brand your website to fit your (first) cover.

See Illustration #1: https://broterandbeatty.com/illustrations-for-authors-tool-kit/#illu1

Here is another example: You are an entrepreneur who has developed a proprietary method in your field of expertise on which you have based your business and offers. You have already developed a visual brand profile for the business and method, and your website and other visual touchpoints are all designed according to this. Then, you put your method into writing and publish it as a book with the same title as your method. Should the book cover be designed within the existing visual profile? YES. Because it is part of your business and existing visual brand.

See Illustration #2: https://broterandbeatty.com/illustrations-for-authors-tool-kit/#illu2

Let's look at the two different kinds of visual branding we must consider as authors:

Book Covers Branded to Each Book

Your book covers are essential visual touchpoints for your author brand. People will probably see your cover before they see your website. Books should be branded to themselves and reflect the content of the book. Here are the key points that I will be covering in this part:

Your Book Cover Is a Mini Billboard

- Your cover should be branded to the book itself—not your author brand.
- It should be recognizable at a thumbnail size (think Amazon search results).
- The imagery, typography, and colors should communicate the genre and mood of the book.

I could write in length on what you should consider when having your book cover designed. In the format of this anthology, I will provide you with some key points on parameters and style.

Parameters for Book Cover Design

- **We live in a world of thumbnails**. People have changed how they buy books. Neither on websites like Amazon nor in online advertising will people see your book cover in 1:1 size. This means that the most important condition your book cover must meet, is that of being able to withstand downscaling without losing its meaning and impact. How do we do that?

- **By using clear figuration**. Clear figuration means an image has a clear motive with as little additional "visual noise" as possible. Clear figuration will let us see the motive of the cover even when downscaled. Having this fact clear in our minds, what's next?

- **The only illustration**. The cover is your sole opportunity to convey something visually. (Unless you are making an illustrated book) This single illustration bears the responsibility of being the overall visual representation of the entire book's content. It is almost like a logo. Your cover should capture and convey the main idea, concept, mood, and associations of your book. The cover should set the tone at a high level, rather than diving into details.

- **Format.** Books can be any format: portrait, landscape, or square. The image or illustration you are looking for needs to fit into the given format. If your book is in a narrow portrait format (6x9 inches) and you want to feature a panoramic view on the cover, you must realize that to include the whole panorama, the photo itself will need to be rendered in a small size and cannot simultaneously cover the 6x9 heightwise.

After examining these parameters, let's proceed to the content. Regardless of *what you plan to depict* on your cover, you can make the design process easier for yourself by first deciding on *how you will depict it*. By that, I mean finding the visual means—such as graphic style, typography, and color—that will effectively support the content of your book. Let's take a look at these means:

Choosing Your Books' Graphic Style, Typography, and Color

Graphic Styles are different ways of depicting the same visual content. You can think of them as visual dialects.

These images all say "bear," but in very different ways. Each of these bears has a context waiting for them, where they will be exactly the right cover image. Try to imagine what kind of book would be found inside a cover with each of these illustrations.

The graphic styles of the bears vary from photorealistic via drawings to cartoonish, and each can be further varied within its style. We can also use humor and metaphors within each style. The possibilities are endless. When deciding on the motif for your book cover and the style in which it will be presented, I recommend having a conversation with your editor and cover designer.

Typography. Your book will need a title on the cover, and the title will need a font. Fonts say more than the words that have been set with them. What do I mean by that? Fonts have strong "flavors" and can evoke associations with specific industries, historical periods, geographical areas, and many other things. Take five seconds to study these examples.

As simple as that	Open Sans
We take up some space!	Montserrat
Back to Britain!	Gill
Formality first	Didot
Secretarial Secrets	american typewriter
Square Up Asap	Orbitron
Ancient auntie	Dashu

Using a font that doesn't suit the words sends out a signal that can be the total opposite of what you want. You will need to test your title in more than one font to see how different fonts affect it. Remember to check how your cover typography holds up when downscaled. How will it look like in a thumbnail? Very thin and elaborate fonts don't downscale well.

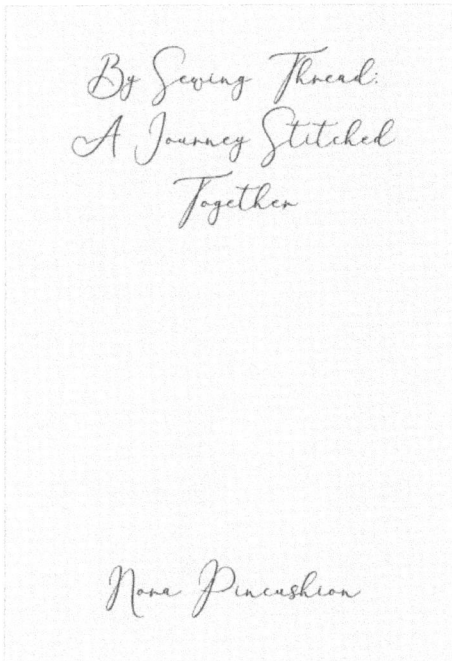

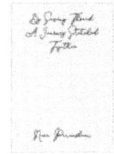

Your cover can be typography only, don't forget that! Many best-sellers have only letters on their covers! If you choose to have typo-graphic art on your cover, leave it to a professional designer to create it.

Book Cover Colors. We have already discussed how you can choose a graphic style, an image, and a font that represents the idea and mood of your book. Now, we need to complete the cover with colors that will work well with the other elements and even enhance them. If your cover art does not span the entire cover, you need to find colors that work well with the art for the areas that are not occupied by the photo or illustration. You'll also need to find colors for the text and back cover.

One way to find colors that work well with a photo or illustration is to select them directly from the image itself. It is a good idea to pick two to three colors from the photo/illustration and create a color palette that can be used consistently across the cover.

See Illustration #3: https://broterandbeatty.com/illustrations-for-authors-tool-kit/#illu3

A Tip About the Back Cover. I recommend you print and measure your back cover. WHY? Unlike the front cover, which needs to work in smaller sizes than we created it, your back cover needs to be readable when people hold it in their hands. When you print the back cover, you will discover if the text is too small or perhaps too big. If your book is 6 x 9 inches, use a ruler to ensure that what comes out of your printer is actually 6 x 9 inches. If you have left the settings in your printer to "scale to fit," it will scale the cover to use the entire paper in your printer, which is 8.5 x 11 inches. As a result, your back cover will emerge from the printer, looking like something for the visually impaired. Set your printer to 100 percent.

The Author Brand

We have looked at how the design of book cover(s) is an important part of author branding because it is through them that your audience will meet you first and foremost. So, what about this "author brand" I am talking about? Where will we use that?

Consider your author brand to be a container for your books. You will use it on your author website, in your email newsletters, and in promotional materials that feature one or more of your books or promote you as an author. Since it is most likely that all these touchpoints will feature one or more of your book covers, your author brand should not visually "fight" for attention with them but constitute a supporting background for any cover. Consequently, the visual means, and especially color, should be neutral.

Author brand elements are:

- Signature logo
- Neutral color palette
- Brand Font

Let's look at these one by one.

Signature Logo: Four Different Kinds

- Some authors want their signature logo to consist of their name only, written in a straightforward manner in their author brand font. Depending on the length of your name, you can consistently render it on one or two lines wherever it is used or let the context and space in which it is rendered decide this. In any case, the consistent visual branding will still be the font.

- Another solution some authors prefer is to let the signature logo have one or more significant custom-created typographic twists, like combining two letters into one, swapping a dot over an I with a tiny symbol, or adding a "swash" to an ending letter. These custom typographic variations are easier to understand when you see them; please see the illustration below.

- Some authors prefer a more comprehensive logo accompanied by a companion logo icon and a tagline. A tagline will highlight this, especially when the logo owner is not only an author but also promotes themselves in other roles, such as a speaker, editor, mentor, podcaster, or teacher.

- In some genres, authors and publishers may prefer to use the author's logo on the front cover instead of setting the author's name in the same font as the title, subtitle, and back cover text. Discuss this with your publisher, book coach, or designer.

Author Brand Neutral Color Palette

Neutral colors that won't clash with colorful covers can be found in the gray-tone spectrum. The gray-tone spectrum/range/scale contains the colors that span between white and black; in other words, all grays you can think of, from light to dark. All colors within this spectrum/range/scale are NEUTRAL; that is, they will not clash or fight with colorful book covers.

Any color will "step down" from dominance if rendered with a low saturation. They are then perceived as "pale" or gray versions of themselves.

Please see the companion PDF, where I suggest some neutral color palettes.

Author Brand Font

The font of an author's brand should also be low-key but with sufficient significance to provide recognition. Please refrain from using noisy display fonts or fonts with elaborate typographical details. These will draw unwanted attention to themselves, not only from the book cover(s) in the contexts but also from the words that have been set with them. *(I cannot hear what you say because of the way you are saying it)*

See Illustrations 4-7: https://broterandbeatty.com/illustrations-for-authors-tool-kit/#illu4

Let a Graphic Designer Help

When creating your visual author brand, I recommend hiring a graphic designer to assist you. Logo design, color, and typography are their expertise. They can also help you implement your visual branding on the touchpoints where you will be using it and create templates from which you can produce your own materials, such as social media post images, ads, and newsletters. Please see the companion PDF for examples.

Your Author Website

Your visual author branding will, of course, also be used on your author website. In Chapter 3 of this book, you will find information on the content required for your website, along with its recommended order. To give you the most useful illustration of how the book page on an author's website may look, we have built two of them: one for a fiction author's website and another for nonfiction. Links to these examples can be found after the website chapter.

Author Branding vs. Book Branding: Quick Recap

- Your **author brand** is your **professional identity**—your website, social media, and email marketing should reflect this.

- **Each book should have its own branding** to match its genre, mood, and audience expectations.

- Choose **neutral branding elements** (fonts, colors) for your author brand so they don't clash with different book covers.

- **Think long-term!** Your website should support multiple books—not just your first release.

TWO

UnSuckify Your Author Bio

Deborah Kevin, MA

Let's be honest: most author bios are about as exciting as soggy toast. You know the ones—the corporate résumés masquerading as "About the Author" sections, written in stiff third person with a heavy dose of academic credentials and exactly zero personality. These bios do little to help your reader connect with you—and even less to make you memorable.

In a crowded publishing world, your bio is your first and best opportunity to build the "Know-Like-Trust" factor. Readers (and podcast hosts, conference organizers, and journalists) want to know who you are, like you enough to listen, and trust you enough to buy your book—or invite you onto their stage.

Good news: You don't have to sound like a LinkedIn robot. You can make your bio sparkle by following a few simple, transformative guidelines.

The Core Principles of a Strong Author Bio

Avoid "Corporate Speak." Your bio isn't your résumé. It's not about listing degrees, titles, or awards in chronological order (unless you can do it with flair). Save the formal bullet points for your CV.

Sucky Example:
Jane Flugel graduated summa cum laude from Florida State University with a degree in psychology. After working in the corporate world for twenty-seven years as a clinical psychologist, Jane launched her own coaching business, Head-Shrinkers, which helps middle-aged women tap into their power and take decisive action.

Keep It Conversational. Your bio should sound like you're introducing yourself to someone at a (fun) dinner party, not a board meeting. A little voice, a little humor, and a little humanity go a long way.

UnSuckified Example:
When Jane Flugel rappelled down the side of Mount Rushmore and felt a burst of adrenaline, she knew she could no longer be held captive by "The Man." Shedding her clinical psychology practice of twenty-seven years, Jane launched *HeadShrinkers*, a coaching business for middle-aged women transitioning from "meh" to "Shazam!"

Notice: We get a glimpse of her *spirit*, not just her credentials.

Share Your Philosophy. What do you stand for? Why do you write, coach, teach, or create? Weave your why into your bio.

Example:
Driven by the belief that women over forty are just getting started, Jane Flugel helps her clients toss out societal expectations and claim lives that feel downright exhilarating.

Highlight What Makes You Unique. Anyone can list credentials. Few can showcase their soul. Highlight the juicy details that make you, *you*.

Example:
When she's not helping women rediscover their badassery, Jane can be found chasing thunderstorms, writing country songs about self-reinvention, or learning Italian—one badly pronounced phrase at a time.

Show (Strategic) Vulnerability. Readers love authenticity. A little glimpse of imperfection makes you *relatable*, not weak.

Example:
Jane once missed a TED Talk audition because she was convinced she had nothing "new" to say. Turns out, her story was exactly what thousands needed to hear.

Be Crystal Clear About What You Offer. Readers should know, without squinting, what you do and for whom.

Example:
Jane Flugel coaches women in midlife who feel stuck, supporting them to reignite their passions, reclaim their dreams, and rock their next chapter.

Bio Templates to Get You Started

Here's a simple structure to help you build your best bio:

[First Name] [Last Name] is a [your role] who [what you do and for whom]. A [philosophy or belief], [First Name] [quirky fact, vulnerability, or relatable moment]. When not [working], [First Name] can be found [personal details that show personality].

More "Before and After" Examples

Example 1: From "Blah" to "Brilliant." Sometimes, an author bio reads like a LinkedIn profile accidentally wandered into a creative space. The information might be technically correct, but it does nothing to spark a connection. In this first example, you'll see how a perfectly "fine" bio can become fabulous with a few simple, strategic shifts in voice, tone, and detail.

Before:
Susan Martinez holds a master's in education and has spent twenty years working in secondary school administration. She enjoys curriculum development and public speaking.

After:
After twenty years of wrangling teenagers and rewriting endless lesson plans, Susan Martinez realized her real passion wasn't just education—it was storytelling. Today, she empowers educators to reclaim their creativity through workshops, keynotes, and her debut book, *Chalk Dust Dreams*. When she's not championing teacher voices, you'll find her hiking with her rescue dog, Winston, or binge-watching historical dramas with a giant mug of coffee in hand.

Example 2: From "Dry" to "Delightful." Credentials are important, yes—but *personality* is what makes an author unforgettable. In this second example, watch how we transform a bland, fact-heavy bio into one that tells a mini-story, shows vulnerability, and invites readers into the author's world. Your audience wants a guide they trust, not a robot with certificates!

Before:
Mark Hughes is a leadership consultant with fifteen years of experience in the tech industry. He holds certifications from Harvard Business School.

After:
Mark Hughes once led a team that accidentally blew a hole through an office ceiling—and learned more about leadership that day than in fifteen years of seminars. Today, he

helps executives navigate the messiness of leadership with humor, humility, and hard-won wisdom. His book, *Leaders Who Don't Duck*, delivers no-fluff strategies for showing up when the stakes are sky-high. When he's not coaching CEOs, Mark plays blues guitar (badly) and obsesses over barbecue competitions.

First-Person vs. Third-Person Bios

When writing your author bio, it's important to match the voice to the platform where it will appear. Generally, first-person bios—where you say "I"—work best for personal spaces like your website, social media profiles, and podcast appearances. First-person writing builds immediate intimacy and trust, making readers feel like they're having a real conversation with you. It sounds warm, approachable, and authentic. For example:

> *I'm Jane Flugel—a recovering corporate psychologist who now helps women flip the script on midlife mediocrity.*

On the other hand, third-person bios—where you refer to yourself by name—are the professional standard for book covers, speaker introductions, event programs, and media kits. Third-person language sounds more polished and formal, which is especially helpful when someone else is quoting or introducing you. It keeps things consistent and easy to use for event organizers or press contacts. Here's how that might look:

> *Jane Flugel is a midlife coach and speaker who helps women reignite their dreams after forty.*

Both formats have their place in your toolkit; the key is using the one that best fits the situation while maintaining your unique voice and presence.

How Many Bios (and What Length)?

Smart authors don't have just one bio—they have a small *arsenal* ready to go. Different opportunities call for different word counts and tones, and having your bios prepared ahead of time saves you stress when an event organizer, podcast host, or media outlet needs one *yesterday*. Ideally, you should have at least three versions of your author bio on hand:

- **Short Bio (50–75 words).** This is your quick introduction for event programs, podcast guesting, panel appearances, or the back cover of a book. It should capture your essence and highlight your core message in a single paragraph.

- **Medium Bio (100–150 words).** Perfect for your website About page, guest blog posts, or speaking proposals. This version gives a little more space to weave in personality, philosophy, and credentials without overwhelming the reader.

- **Long Bio (200–300 words).** This version is useful for press kits, speaker one-sheets, or media interviews where a deeper background is helpful. It can include a touch more storytelling: why you do what you do, who you serve, and even a hint about your passions or personal life.

Pro Tip: Save all three versions of your bio in one easy-to-access folder (Google Drive, Dropbox, or your desktop), clearly labeled by length. Bonus points if you include both first-person and third-person options for each! Future-you will thank you when opportunities pop up. Having these ready positions you as professional, prepared, and polished—and ensures you'll always sound like your best self, no matter where your words take you.

Final Tips for Your Author Bio

- Update it regularly as your career evolves.
- Match the tone to your brand: playful, bold, wise, soulful.
- Use powerful, specific verbs ("helps," "guides," "creates," "inspires").
- Keep it between **75–150 words** unless instructed otherwise.
- Invite connection! You want readers thinking, *I want to know more.*

In Short?

Your bio isn't just about you. It's about *who you are to your reader.* Let them see the magic. Let them feel the pull. UnSuckify your bio— and watch your audience grow.

THREE

Author Website

Sandra Beatty with Cheri D. Andrews, Esq.

You just finished a riveting book you couldn't put it down. And now you want to know more about the author. You Google their name only to find... nothing. No website, no information, just a lonely Amazon page.

If readers can't find and learn more about you, they can't become fans. Whether you're a new or established author, you need to have a place to send people who want to purchase your book. You have several options to consider:

- Physical bookstores
- Online bookstores
- Your website

Physical Bookstore Locations

You could tell people to go to their local bookstore, but your reach is limited with this option. They might not be close to a bookstore or their local bookstore might not carry your book. Perhaps they don't want a physical copy of your book but prefer digital.

This option only works for a particular (shrinking) segment of people who are close to a bookstore; they visit it regularly, want a physical copy, and will ask their local bookstore to order your book if it's not available on the shelves. This is, of course, on the assumption that they even know your book exists.

Of all the purchasing options, this one is likely to result in the fewest sales.

Online Bookstores

The next best thing is to have your book available online in markets like Amazon, Barnes & Noble, Bookshop.org, and such. With this avenue, your book is far more accessible, it can be purchased in digital and hard copy formats, and if certain conditions are met, it can be promoted as a bestseller and put in front of new potential readers and buyers.

The downsides?

These sites promote different offerings. All. The. Time. The health of their business is directly tied to the price tag of a shopper's cart. And so, they promote items they think shoppers will buy based on their previous buying histories. This can cause problems for you because humans are easily sidetracked and might choose to buy something else instead of your book. Ugh.

You also have to work within the limitations of their fields. Consequently, you can't add promotional bonuses or external links to connect with your readers.

Compared to physical bookstore locations, you'll definitely get more sales with this option.

But if you want to establish yourself as a credible, professional author (and increase your book sales), there's something else you need to add to your toolkit.

Your Website

With your website, you have total control over everything, including how it looks and what is written. You can add the best testimonials … and keep adding them.

You can add a variety of purchase options to your site to appeal to all your readers. You can add bonuses and remove them when the promotion is over. And it's relatively easy to update and change— once you know what you're doing.

It's like having your own digital house to design as you please without the expensive price tag.

But I won't sugarcoat this—creating a website is time-consuming, especially if you've never done it before. However, if you already have a website, updating it should be easier because you already have some basic, essential things in place.

But before we get into all that, there's something you must answer first.

Before Starting, Answer This Critical Question

There is one obvious thing you need to remember whether or not you already have a website. It's this: The ultimate purpose of your website is to influence visitors to *buy your book*.

In order to achieve that goal, you must understand buyer psychology. People buy books because they're looking for something *they* want or need. Not what *you* want or need. In other words, their reasons for purchasing your book are about them, not you.

So, if you want more book sales, your website needs to answer some version of this question: How will your book benefit me (as the potential reader)?

Your answers might be:

- A debt-free life
- Avoid painful mistakes
- An escape from your current reality

Whatever the answer, you'll have the best chance of more book sales if you can clearly articulate how your book will make your reader's life better.

To the best of your ability, answer one (or all) of the below questions first before writing (or rewriting) the words for your website.

The purpose of this exercise is to persuade your reader to buy your book! So don't go for the obvious answer—dig a little deeper and see how far you can go:

- How will your book benefit me?
- How will your book make my life better?
- What problem does your book solve for me?

Your Book Template to Maximize Book Sales

First, a caveat: How to create a website is a *ginormous* topic—too big to get into within this anthology. And there are two audiences reading this book:

1. Those who don't have a website and want to establish themselves as a credible author (and increase book sales).
2. Those who already have a website and need to refresh or upgrade their site.

What's included herein will work with both audiences.

The Most Important Page of Your Website

Instead of talking about an entire website, I'm going to focus on THE most important page of your site—*the page that sells your book*—because it's applicable to both audiences.

- **If you don't have a website**, I want to put your mind at ease—a one-page website will work just fine. (For context, a one-page website doesn't have additional pages, such as an About page or Contact page or such. It's only one page, hence why it's called a one-page website.) You're going to use your one-page website to sell your book.
- **If you have a website**, you can apply what I'm about to teach to the page(s) that is selling your book(s).

There are two sections below—one for nonfiction and the other for fiction. Choose which one applies to you. Let's get started!

Overwhelmed? Start small. You don't need a complex website. A one-page book website is enough to start building your author brand!

NONFICTION BOOK PAGE

First, Gather Information

For an easier and more successful execution, first, gather the following pieces of information so they're accessible. You might not have all of them, and that's okay. Do your best with what you have:

1. Answer: How is your book going to benefit me, the reader? If possible, include in your answer who your book is for.
2. Trust and authority signals: Awards, "Featured in" logos, education (if this information is important to your audience).
3. Social proof: Testimonials and reviews.
4. Answer: What is your reader's pain/problem/desired outcome that your book helps them achieve?
5. Answer: How is your reader's pain/problem/unrealized desired outcome negatively impacting their life?
6. Description/summary of your book. Include a list of six things in your book that will help your reader address their pain/problem/desired outcome.
7. Author bio.
8. Free bonuses (if using).
9. Free resources (if using).

Second, Write the Words

You need something that's as easy as possible for you to implement *and* that gives you the best chance of book sales. The template below will help you do just that. Each section in the template has at least one specific question that needs to be answered.

> **Section 1 (Hero Section) Answers:** Who is this book for? How will this book benefit me? What will I get from your book? *Include a call-to-action button that essentially calls them to buy*

> **Credibility and Authority Banner Answers:** Why should I trust you/your competency as an expert? Use what you gathered for the trust signals (#2) and/or social proof (#3).

> **Section 2: Call Out Their Problem, Pain, or Desire to Answer:** What is the problem, pain, or desire of your prospective reader? Draw upon the answer you provided to item #4 above.

> **Section 3: Agitate Their Pain and Answers:** How is their life being negatively affected? Draw upon the answer you provided to item #5 above.

> **Section 4: Introduce Your Book as the Solution and Answers:** How will your book bring relief/solution/closure to their problem/pain/desire? Include a call-to-action button. Draw upon the answer you provided above to items #6 and #10.

> **Social Proof Banner (Testimonials and Ratings) Answers:** What are people saying about your book? Use what you gathered above for the trust signals (#2) and/or social proof (#3).

> **Section 5: Your Author Bio Answers:** Why should I trust you/your competency as an expert?

Section 6: Remind Them How to Your Book Benefits Them and How to Purchase, and Answers: What are the benefits of buying your book? (This is a good place for your bonuses or free resources.) Include a call-to-action button.

It can be difficult to understand how writing for each section will translate into a web page. I get it. A picture is worth a thousand words, right?

You can see a mock-up of a sample book here: https://broterandbeatty.com/non-fiction-book-page/

FICTION BOOK PAGE

A book web page for a fiction book has very similar elements as a non-fiction book but doesn't need to be as lengthy.

First, Gather Information
For an easier and successful execution, first gather the following pieces of information so they're accessible (You might not have all of them and that's okay. Do your best with what you have.):

1. Trust and authority signals: Awards, "Featured on" logos.
2. Social proof: Advance reader blurbs and post-publishing reviews.
3. Description/summary of your book.
4. SWAG (if using): bookmarks, autographed bookplate, book club questions, stickers (See Chapter 8).
5. Author bio (See Chapter 2).

Second, Write the Words
You need something that's as easy to implement as possible and that

will give you the best chance of book sales. The template below will help you do just that. Each section in the template has at least one specific question that needs to be answered.

Section 1 (Hero Section) Answers: What is this book about? Why should I buy your book? Include a call-to-action button that essentially calls them to buy. Draw upon items from #1, 2, 3, and 4 above.

Credibility and Authority Banner Answers: Why should I trust you/your competency as a fictional writer? Use items you gathered in #1 and #2.

Section 2: Book Description Answers: Does this appeal to me? Do I want to read it? Draw upon your answer to #3.

Social Proof Banner (Testimonials and Ratings) Answers: What are people saying about your book? Use items you gathered in #1 and #2.

Section 3: Your Author Bio Answers: What is your writing experience? What are you like? (People want to know more about you and might look for commonalities they share with you, such as loving dogs, drinking a particular brand of coffee, etc.) Draw upon your answer to #5.

Social Proof Banner (Testimonials and Ratings) Answers: What are people saying about your book? Use items you gathered in #2.

Optional Section: A Free Sample of Your Book Answers: How do I know I'm going to enjoy this book?

Social Proof Banner (Testimonials and Ratings) Answers: What are people saying about your book? Use items you gathered in #2. Add this banner if you're putting in the Free Sample optional section above.

Section 4: Remnder Them How to Your Book Benefits Them and How to Purchase, and Answers: Why should I buy your book? (This is a good place for your bonuses or SWAG.) Include buttons for where they can buy the book (e.g., Amazon, Bookshop.org, Barnes & Noble, etc.). Draw upon items to #4.

For an example of applying the template to a sample fiction book web page, go to https://broterandbeatty.com/fiction-book/.

Beware of Common Mistakes

As you write your book page, avoid these common pitfalls could negatively impact your book sales:

- **Too Much About You, Not Enough About the Reader.** Keep the focus on answering the question on your reader's mind—*Why should I buy your book?*
- **Hiding Your Book Link.** Readers should never have to hunt for the "Buy" button!
- **Too Much Information.** Humans tend to get overwhelmed, or lose interest, if information is too detailed. Ask yourself, *"Is this information going to help the reader buy my book?"*
- **Paragraphs Too Long.** Break up text with images, bullet points, subheadings, and bolded words. White space helps readers engage with your book page.
- **Uninteresting Hero Section.** One hundred percent of your visitors will see the hero section and, based on what they see, decide whether to scroll further. This is

your one opportunity to WOW them! Make your hero section interesting and persuasive.

Choosing Your Website Platform

There are so many website platforms available—and the possibilities grow each year.

As well, the requirements of technical expertise to use the platforms vary. For those reasons, it's best that you decide what is best for you. Here is a simple self-assessment quiz you can take to help you narrow down your options:

Step 1: Self-Assessment—How Tech-Savvy are you?
Choose the statement that sounds most like you:

A. "I want something simple. Just let me pick a template and get it done."

B. "I'm okay learning a little bit or tweaking settings, especially if I get more control."

C. "I'm comfortable with plugins, themes, and maybe even some code—or I've got help."

If you picked A: Go with a non-tech platform. If you picked B: Look at somewhat-tech options. If you picked C: Look at tech-savvy options.

Step 2: What Do You Want Your Website to Do?
Decide what you want your website to do based on the options across the top of the table below. The far-left column is the most common website platforms and their ranges of technical savviness needed to use them.

This simple self-assessment will help you narrow down your options based on the features you want and the level of your technical skills.

NON-TECHY	SHOWCASE YOUR BOOKS	BLOG	SELL BOOKS DIRECTLY	CREATIVE CONTROL	FAST, ONE-PAGE SITE
Weebly	✓	✓	✓	None	
Strikingly	✓		✓	None	✓
Carrd	✓			None	✓

SOMEWHAT TECHY	SHOWCASE YOUR BOOKS	BLOG	SELL BOOKS DIRECTLY	CREATIVE CONTROL	FAST, ONE-PAGE SITE
Wix	✓	✓	✓	Some	
Squarespace	✓	✓	✓	Some	

TECH SAVVY	SHOWCASE YOUR BOOKS	BLOG	SELL BOOKS DIRECTLY	CREATIVE CONTROL	FAST, ONE-PAGE SITE
WordPress	✓	✓	✓	Full	
Ghost	✓	✓		None	
Webflow	✓	✓	✓	Full	

Next Step: Design Your Book Page

You've gathered the information you need to write your book web page. You've written the copy for your book web page using one of the templates above as a guide. Now, you need to *design* your book web page so it's visually appealing and establishes you as a credible, professional author.

In Chapter 1, Hanne Brøter wrote about how to apply graphic design to your brand and touched on applying it to your author website. Refer to Hanne's chapter for design principles you'll need to follow for your website.

Website Legal Compliance: The Privacy Policy

As you are building your totally kick-ass author website, don't forget to add a privacy policy so your site is legally compliant!

A privacy policy is a legal document posted on your website or mobile app that establishes your compliance with consumer privacy regulations. Think of it as an agreement between your company and your website visitors with respect to their personal information.

Do you really need a privacy policy? Well, if your website is a static site for information only AND has no forms for collecting names, emails, or other personal information for email marketing, scheduling purposes, or to enable download of a lead magnet or purchase of your book AND you have turned OFF all cookies, pixels, and other methods of collecting metrics, then you might not NEED a privacy policy.

BUT, the data protection agencies EXPECT to see a privacy policy on every website. You may be drawing unwanted attention (and possibly data audits) to your website with the lack of one.

If your website has or will have a lead magnet, newsletter sign up, scheduler, or contact form that you use to obtain names, emails, or phone numbers or collects metrics like clicks, views, or IP addresses, or you are selling your book from your website, then you **NEED** a **privacy policy!**

Why? Because when you are collecting names, emails, phone numbers, addresses, payment information, and metrics, what you are collecting is personal information. Which means you are required to have a privacy policy under the GDPR (EU's General Data Protection Regulations) & the laws of many states in the United States. Even if you don't do business in those places – You can't prevent a visitor from EU or one of those states from entering information on your site. And the minute they do, those laws kick in. Your website visitors have the right to know what you collect, why you collect it, and how they can get it removed from your database.

The information that must be included in a privacy policy includes:

- WHAT information you collect (names, emails, IP addresses, etc.);
- WHEN you collect (when they visit, when they fill out a form, place an order);
- WHY you collect it (to fulfill an order, to send a download, to subscribe to a newsletter);

- WHO you share it with—it is a good practice to include all third-party plug-ins such as Google Analytics or other metrics services, third-party payment processors, social media sites, email marketing platforms, etc.;
- WHETHER you sell it and to whom;
- HOW long you store it and how you protect it—this is to ensure your data retention and data security measures are in place; and
- WHERE you can be contacted to request access, modification, or deletion of personal data.

To ensure that your privacy policy is compliant with GDPR and state laws, I urge you to work with an attorney to create a privacy policy that is customized for your author business. While you are at it, ask about a terms of use. This is the agreement with your website visitors about how they can and cannot use the information on your website, and it provides a lot of legal protections for you!

FOUR

Understanding Copyright

Cheri D. Andrews, Esq.

Copyright is a confusing topic. And no small wonder since it defies all the "rules" of other types of intellectual property!

But before we dig into exactly what copyright is and why it is important to you as an author, I want to get one distinction straight. Copyright (notice it ends with the word "right") as it is used here is the bundle of intellectual property rights that automatically attach to creative expression. It should not be confused with copywrite (notice it ends with the word "write"), which literally means the act of writing copy such as advertisements, blog posts, and articles for marketing and social media, usually on someone else's behalf.

What is Copyright?

Copyright is the bundle of exclusive intellectual property rights granted by law to the creator of creative expression with respect to their work. These rights arise automatically as soon as the creator fixes their creative expression in a tangible medium, known as a "work." These rights include:

- **Reproduction** – literally the right to make copies. This is the most important right a copyright owner gets. This right applies to all types of works.

- **Adaptation** – or "Derivative Works" is the right to use the work to create something new, such as when a novel is adapted to a movie, or a book is translated into another language. As the owner of this right, you can license the ability to adapt your work—this creates some very lucrative downstream market opportunities. Once licensed, the derivative work created may then be eligible to obtain its own copyright protection.

- **Public Distribution** – the right to sell or transfer ownership or rent, lease, lend (or give away) your work to the public at large. Putting your book up on Amazon so people can buy it is public distribution. Public distribution can also include giving away copies of your book, selling it via your own website or other bookstores, etc. The right of public distribution protects the copyright owner against the distribution of infringing copies.

- **Public Display** – the right to show the work in public. In a bookstore, a shelf with your books sitting on it is an act of display, although this right more typically refers to things like displaying a painting or sculpture in a museum or gallery.

- **Public Performance** – typically when we think of public performance, we think of the right to perform a play on Broadway or show a movie in a theater. In the case of your book, public performance would be the right to do a public reading.

- **Digital/Audio Transmission** – the right to broadcast a work to the public. This includes radio, television, and podcasting. It does not apply to literary or artistic works.

How Long Does Your Copyright Last?

The exclusive rights mentioned above continue for the life of the creator plus seventy years. So, you can pass your copyright to your heirs and they can continue to receive royalties, license the work, and take advantage of these rights. After that, your work goes into the public domain.

Because your copyright can last seventy years beyond your death, it may be appropriate to name beneficiaries for your copyrighted works. If your work is still selling well, you may wish to create a literary estate. In this case, in addition to your standard will provisions, you will have provisions dealing specifically with your copyrighted works. We'll talk more about literary estates a bit later.

What Does Copyright Protect?

Copyright protects **original works of authorship fixed in a tangible medium**, including literary, dramatic, musical, and artistic works. The protection covers the author's **creative expression**, but not the facts or ideas underlying that expression. That is a lot to try to comprehend, so I want to unpack each element of copyright for you in order to help you understand.

Elements of Copyright

"**Original work of authorship**" means the work must embody a modicum or "spark" of creativity **and** the work must "originate" with the author as an independent creation, not as a copy from something already existing.

Case law tells us that for a work to qualify as an "original work of authorship" the creative expression must be made by a **human** and the spark of creativity requires more than just manual labor.

The "human" requirement was the subject of a famous lawsuit between the animal rights activist group PETA and British nature photographer David Slater. Slater claimed copyright ownership of photos taken on his camera, but actually snapped by a macaque—the famous "monkey selfie." To be fair, Mr. Slater did all the work of setting up the camera, and figuring out camera angles and lighting. Only then were the monkeys able to press the shutter button to snap the photos.

PETA claimed the monkey should own the copyright. The 9th Circuit Court of Appeals held that the Copyright Act doesn't permit non-humans to file lawsuits for infringement.[1] Indeed, *The Copyright Office Practices Manual* states that: "The term 'authorship' implies that a work must owe its origin to a human being. Materials produced solely by nature, by plants, or by animals are not copyrightable." Currently, the US Copyright Office requires that authors disclaim any portion of a work created with "appreciable" assistance from AI because it doesn't originate from a human. The law is still evolving in this area.

The "**spark of creativity**" requirement was explained in the case of Feist Publications, Inc. v. Rural Telephone Service Company. Rural Telephone published a telephone directory in a limited region of Northwest Kansas. Feist Publications, on the other hand, published telephone directories with much broader geography. Feist sought to license Rural Telephone's white pages listings for its directory, but Rural Telephone refused to grant them a license. So, Feist extracted the listing information from the white pages without Rural Telephone's consent to include in its directory.

The legal battle that ensued went all the way to the Supreme Court. In 1991 the Supreme Court held that the names, towns, and telephone numbers copied by Feist were not **original** to Rural (they were facts/data) and therefore were not protected by copyright.[2] In doing so, the court reasoned that Rural's white pages did not satisfy the **originality** requirement, as Rural had not selected, coordinated, or arranged the uncopyrightable facts in any unique way, failing to show the requisite spark of creativity.

"**Fixed in a tangible medium**" means that you take the expression of your thoughts and ideas out of your head and record them in some manner. A photographic image exists on the drive of your camera or cell phone. A blog post exists as a file on your website page. A painting is created on a canvas. A sculpture is modeled in clay. And your book is recorded on paper or in a word processing file on your computer. These all qualify as being "fixed in a tangible medium."

"**Creative Expression**" is the sole domain of copyright law. Copyright protects your creative ideas that are **expressed** in some format.

Copyright does **not** protect ideas—it protects the creative expression of those ideas. If the ideas are still in your head, there is no copyright protection. If you share your ideas with someone else in a conversation, there is no copyright protection, unless you happen to record the conversation because, remember, the expression must be fixed in a tangible medium.

Copyright also does **not** protect facts or data. For example, if you write a blog post comparing three different email marketing platforms, the underlying **facts** such as the names of the platforms, the features on each, and the price of the service are **not** protected by copyright. Anyone can visit your website and freely take and reuse that information. What is protected is the creative expression. This includes the words you use to describe the user experience with the platform, how it operates, and your arrangement of the pros and cons of each platform.

Now that you understand the basics of copyright, you probably have a lot of questions about how it applies to you as an author. Let's see if we can answer a few of them!

The Author's Copyrightable Assets

As an author, do you even have copyrightable assets? Of course you do! There are so many assets you create as an author that are potentially subject to copyright protection. These include:

- Marketing copy for your book
- Website copy for your author page or book landing page
- Blog posts
- Videos for Facebook Live, Instagram, TikTok, LinkedIn, etc.
- Books, eBooks, Audiobooks
- Articles for magazines and newspapers
- Graphics posted to social media
- Images

As long as you are the creator, these all qualify as original works of authorship fixed in a tangible medium. They are all subject to copyright protection.

Protecting Your Copyrightable Assets

You want to take proactive measures to ensure that the rights in your intellectual property assets are protected. The best protection is copyright registration. But if you are a creative soul and have a lot of different content, copyright registration for every piece of content can quickly become time- and cost-prohibitive. Here are some steps you can take immediately short of registering a copyright:

- **Use a Copyright Notice.** Despite the fact that a copyright notice is not legally required, I advise my clients to use a copyright notice on **everything** they create. People tend to believe (wrongly) that anything on the internet is fair game. Your copyright notice tells them your material is **not** fair game. Update the copyright notice on your website yearly. Your copyright notice looks like this: © Your Company Name 2021–2024.

- **Set up Google alerts** for text-based materials. You can create an alert for a block of text from your book or blog post and Google will let you know if it shows up somewhere else.

- **Watermark images, PDFs, etc.** Honestly, the only purpose of this is to make it harder for others to steal and use them, but I'm all for slowing thieves down whenever possible.

- **Hire a copyright monitoring service.** Services such as copyrighted.com or dmca.com will send out a web "spy" to crawl the internet for your content for around $120/year.

What to Do If Someone Infringes

If you learn that someone else is using your work without your permission, you have a few options on how to address it.

- **Ignore it**. If you feel it is okay for anyone to use your work for their own benefit, it is okay to let it go. In some cases, free and open distribution is desired, even if you don't get credit.

- Send a **Digital Millennium Copyright Act (DMCA) take-down notice** to the internet platform where your copyrighted material appears. For instance, if someone posts an excerpt from your book on Facebook without your permission, you can send a take-down notice to Facebook with proof of your ownership and ask them to remove it.

- Send a **cease and desist letter**. The letter calls out the offender on the inappropriate use of your work and asks them to stop immediately.

- **Offer a license**. Offer the offending party a license to use your work in exchange for a licensing fee and attribution. This can also be part of a cease and desist letter as an alternative to ceasing use.

- File an **infringement lawsuit**. If the cease-and-desist letter isn't effective at stopping infringement, this is the next step. BUT … **you must have your copyright registered with the US Copyright Office before you are able to file a lawsuit.** In the case of Fourth Estate Public Benefit Corp. v. Wall-Street.com LLC,[3] the US Supreme Court held that you must have a valid registration in order to pursue copyright infringement litigation.

The Fair Use Doctrine

So, let's say that, hypothetically, you have taken proactive action to protect your IP assets, then you find out that someone is using your work without attribution or permission. You send them a politely worded cease and desist letter asking them to stop using your work, and in response, your infringer tells you that they will not cease using your work and claims that their use is fair use. Wait, *whaaaaat* now?

Surprise, not all copying is copyright infringement! Others can freely use your work if it meets the requirements of fair use. The Fair Use Doctrine is a defense against any claim of copyright infringement.

Fair Use is defined in the Copyright Act as reproduction for a limited or transformative purpose such as criticism, comment, news reporting, teaching, scholarship, or research. Fair use also includes parody. Use of your work for these specific purposes is not infringement as long as the use fits the requirements of the Fair Use Doctrine.

Unfortunately, there is no objective test that draws a line in the sand as to what is, or isn't, a fair use. In determining whether a use is "fair use," courts must consider all four of the following factors:

1. **Purpose and Character.** This includes whether the use is commercial or nonprofit. If the use is commercial, (meaning intended to make money), that weighs against fair use. So, if the person stealing your stuff is also using it to further a business endeavor, it will likely **not** be considered fair use. If it is used for criticism, comment, news reporting, teaching, scholarship, or research not designed for profit, there is a lot more leeway. Nonprofit educational use is likely afforded protection under the Fair Use Doctrine.

2. **The Nature of the Copyrighted Work.** Keep in mind that facts aren't subject to copyright. So, if someone pulls facts out of your article and uses them in a new way, that is fair use. However, if they take the creative part of your work—your particular turn of phrase, a drawing, a poem etc.—and use it for their own purposes, it is likely **not** fair use. The more creative the work used, the less likely a finding of fair use.

3. **The Amount or Substantiality.** This refers to the portion used to the work as a whole. Simply put, the less of the work used, the better. If the use quotes a single sentence from a 200-page book, it leans in favor of fair use. If the use copies a full page of a two-page magazine article, it probably won't be protected.

4. **The Effect on Market or Value.** Does the use effect the potential market or value of the copyrighted work? For example, imagine a photographer takes an iconic photo of the Brooklyn Bridge at sunset and plans to license it exclusively to *Time* magazine for a tidy sum. The value of that photograph lies in the fact that it is, as

yet, unpublished. Now imagine a hacker steals the image from the photographer's computer and sells poster-sized prints and greeting cards of that photograph on an e-commerce website. The hacker has substantially diminished the potential market or value of the photograph for the copyright owner. In this case, the use will **not** be considered a fair use.

All of these factors are subjective, so it is difficult to determine in advance whether or not a use is fair. Purpose and market effect are the most important factors and will be given the most weight by the courts.

Keep in mind that the Fair Use Doctrine is a two-way street. While you are busy trying to protect your own IP, be aware of the intellectual property of others. If you wouldn't want a business owner using your work in a specific manner, then you shouldn't be using the work of others that way either! Make sure you have the rights to everything you are using.

∾

FAQ: When Should I Register?

Q: Should I register every blog post or social media graphic?
A: No. That would be time-consuming and costly. But do consider registering high-value or viral blog posts or signature frameworks.

Q: What about my book?
A: YES! I consider registering your book a **must.** Proactive registration secures full rights and enables enforcement.

Q: Can I register multiple items together?
A: Yes. For certain categories (e.g., group blog posts every 90 days). Ask your attorney for specifics.

Q: When should I file?

A: File your registration either shortly before or immediately upon publication of your book.

∿

The Benefits of Copyright Registration

For any asset you are adamant about protecting, you will want to file an application for copyright registration.

Filing for your copyright registration is a **proactive** measure, not a reactive one (Section 412 US Copyright Act). The benefits of proactively filing for copyright registration on your book (or other copyrightable material) include the ability to sue in federal court and the ability to claim statutory damages and attorney's fees. Without registration, if you discover infringement, you will have to go through the filing process and wait until your copyright is registered to be able to file suit. During this time, your infringer may continue using and benefiting from your copyrighted material.

The beauty of statutory damages is that the court determines the amount of damages without the copyright owner having to prove **actual** damages. Statutory damages are usually between $750 and $30,000 per work but can be increased up to $150,000 per work if you can prove the infringement was intentional.

Actual damages, on the other hand, are difficult to prove, require expert witness testimony, and can be quite expensive to establish. The copyright holder has the burden of proving their actual damages, which may include profit that the copyright owner lost as a result of the infringement (for example, a license fee or royalty income) as well as any additional profits the infringer received as a result of the infringement. The ability to claim statutory damages saves copyright owners from the difficult task of providing evidence of actual damages. (Section 504 US Copyright Act.)

Filing a Copyright Registration

I recommend you hire an attorney versed in the ins and outs of copyright registration to file on your behalf. There are too many potential pitfalls in the system for the unwary. But if you are the consummate DIYer, here are the basic steps:

1. Set up an account with the Electronic Copyright Office at https://eservice.eco.loc.gov.
2. Log in to your account.
3. From the left navigation menu, choose the type of work you wish to register.
4. Complete the application.
5. Pay the fee.
6. Upload or mail your deposit copy(ies) of your work. Deposit copies vary for the type of work.

There are different application forms, and different information is required for each type of work you register. There are also different rules for deposit copies. A single misstep in choosing the correct application form or filling it out will cause your application to be rejected. If this happens, your filing fees are not refundable, and you will need to start the process from scratch.

Once filed, the process for the US Copyright Office to review your application and send you a registration certificate can take up to six months or more. For this reason, proactive filing is the best way to ensure you are ready to move forward expeditiously if you discover someone is infringing your copyrighted works.

∿

Quick Copyright Checklist for Authors

- Add a copyright notice to your website and all your marketing materials, including lead magnets and course materials.

- Watermark high-value images or PDFs.
- Use Google Alerts or a monitoring service to monitor and protect key content.
- Register the copyright for your book shortly before or immediately upon publication.
- Learn how to issue a DMCA takedown notice when your material appears on platforms like Facebook, Instagram, or other social media sites.
- Send cease and desist letters when needed.
- Be aware of what qualifies as *fair use*—for yourself and others.
- Ensure that you have the rights to all materials you use— either because you created it or appropriately licensed it.

Don't wait until your work is stolen to protect it!

Engaging Your Readers

FIVE

The Author's Social Media Toolkit

Jennifer Nichols

Publishing your book is only the beginning! You hit "publish," your book is out in the world—and you brace yourself for the flood of readers, the buzz, the breakthrough. But instead? Silence. But this isn't the end of your author's journey; it is the beginning. Because today, visibility means everything, and without it, your book risks becoming a well-kept secret that collects dust in the garage. Only the beginning? But you've done so much work and poured your heart and soul into this book, and it's only the beginning? Here's the deal: Many authors, including yourself, dream of seeing their book in readers' hands, sparking conversations, and leaving a lasting impact. But in today's digital world, simply publishing a book isn't enough. Social media plays a crucial role in building an audience ahead of time, creating anticipation, and keeping readers engaged long after your book hits the shelves and digital market.

As an author, writing is golden, yet social media can feel over-whelming. Right? How do you stay true to yourself and your book while also maintaining a strategic approach? A well-thought-out plan holds the answer and keeps things simple—just as you wouldn't write a book without an outline, you shouldn't approach social media without a strategic plan. When done right, your online presence isn't just marketing; it's an extension of your brand and identity as an author. An extension of you that your audience craves.

This chapter will guide you through creating a long-term social media plan, staying authentic in your messaging, and showing up consistently before, during, and after your book launch. By treating your author presence as a business, you set yourself up for long-term success that lasts longer than the day of your book launch.

Create a Long-Term Social Media Plan

Many authors treat social media as something to tackle when they "have time" or "get around to it." But a strong online presence, including visibility and followers, isn't built overnight. In fact, the time to start your social media journey is the same time you start your book. Just as you carefully craft your book's plot, you must outline your social media strategy with intention and authenticity. Planning makes that easier.

Key Components of a Social Media Plan

- **Define Your Goals:** Are you looking to grow your email list, increase book sales, or build a community of engaged readers? Your goals will shape your strategy.

- **Know Your Audience:** Who are your readers? Where do they hang out online (*hint—this is important even if you don't hang out in the same place)? If you write cozy mysteries, your audience may be active on Facebook book groups. If you write YA fantasy, Instagram, and TikTok might be better fits.

Business/ Thought Leader	LinkedIn, YouTube, Instagram
Cozy Mystery	Facebook groups, Goodreads groups, YouTube (#booktube), Instagram (#bookstagram)
Memoir	Facebook, Instagram, TikTok, Goodreads, Your newsletter
Nonfiction/ Personal Growth	Facebook, YouTube (#booktube), Instagram, LinkedIn
Romance	TikTok (BookTok), Instagram, Reddit, YouTube
YA Fantasy	TikTok (BookTok), Instagram, Threads

- **Plan Your Content.** Balance promotional posts with engaging, valuable content. A simple rule: 20 percent promotional, 80 percent engagement-driven.

Promotional = Talking about the book, book launch, invite to newsletter sign up and more.
Engagement = Asking your followers questions, sharing your favorite writing nook, sharing snippets of your writing journey.

- **Batch and Schedule.** Use tools, like Metricool, Meta Business Suite, Later, or OneUp, to plan content in advance so you're not scrambling daily. Batching content helps us focus on the time allotted, with no last-minute rush, and ensures consistency to keep the algorithms happy and working in your favor.

- **Measure and Adjust.** The sooner you start, the more time you'll have to track what works and adjust before launch day if needed. Analytics help you gauge what your audience loves and how they consume content from you. Various long-form, short-form, short/long-form videos, and even memes will help you appeal to a larger audience.

A planned approach makes social media manageable and ensures you're not shouting into the void without direction.

Hint Posting and ghosting is a real thing. Don't do this; stay present and set times to check in and engage with the comments on your posts, as well as commenting on other people's stuff. Fifteen minutes twice a day will improve and make the algorithms happier.

Staying Authentic to Yourself and Your Book

It's easy to get caught up in trends or what an online search tells you to post, but readers connect with authors who feel real. You don't need to dance on TikTok if that's not your style. Authenticity means showing up as yourself—your voice, values, and unique perspective. Show up online for your audience the very same way you would if they met you at a friend's birthday party. At first, it will feel vulnerable; however, sharing who you are invites them to relate to you, trust you, and rely on your messages. Starting months before your book launches allows you to take baby steps and practice authenticity over time.

How to Stay Authentic Online

- **Let Your Book's Theme Guide You.** If your book is

about resilience, weave that into your posts with personal stories, quotes, and even articles you've read.

- **Speak the Way You Write.** If your book is witty and humorous, reflect that in your posts. If it's poetic and introspective, let your social media reflect that tone. Remember, consistency is the key here, too. Your voice matters to the reader online and offline.

- **Engage Genuinely.** Reply to comments, interact with your readers, and show appreciation. Readers who feel a personal connection to you are more likely to become loyal fans.

- **Set Boundaries.** Share what you're comfortable with. If you don't want to post personal life details, focus on your writing journey, book research, or industry insights.

Sample Content Ideas

- If writing a rom-com, you could create a post that asks to share with your online audience "How my character would flirt vs. how I flirt (spoiler alert: One of us needs help)."
- Is your book a Hallmark-type romance? Consider sharing posts of photos with content that says, "things that inspire my happily-ever-afters."
- For mystery/thriller authors, you can create social media posts that keep your followers guessing what happens next. Posts like, "This sentence (insert sentence) will make sense after Chapter 9.
- Memoirs offer a chance to connect with your online audience through a 'then vs. now' style post, revealing personal growth, mindset shifts, or beliefs changes.

Your social media presence feels natural rather than forced when you remain authentic. This not only makes it easier for you to maintain, but also attracts the right readers.

Showing Up Before, During, and After the Book Launch

Social media isn't just about the launch day—it's about the long game. Many authors make the mistake of only showing up when they have something to sell. Your audience needs to see you consistently, not just in promotional bursts. You are always selling YOU and your brand. Don't create an environment where your followers and readers feel you only show up when you want something from them.

Before the Launch

- Share your writing journey (drafting struggles, inspiration, behind-the-scenes glimpses).
- Reveal your book cover or a few cover options and ask for opinions, share the title, advance copy unboxing videos, and snippets to build anticipation.
- Start engaging with potential readers, book bloggers, and fellow authors.
- Ideally, this should start six months before the book is published.

During the Launch

- Host a virtual book party or Q&A session.
- Share reader testimonials, early reviews, video interviews with those who were advanced readers, and videos of you reading a paragraph or more.
- Create energy and excitement with limited-time bonuses when possible, posts from launch partners, flat swag or signed copies. *Hint* Answer this question when posting: "What will get them to buy today instead of someday?"

After the Launch

- Keep the momentum going with book-related content (deleted segments, you taking a break after launch, revisiting some of the fun or challenging creation aspects, character deep dives, author reflections).
- Continue engaging with readers and building your brand for future books.
- Repurpose content to attract new readers (pull quotes, blog posts, guest podcast appearances).
- Remember to ask for reviews, too. Often, people need to be told how they can help or what to do next.

By showing up consistently, you establish yourself as an author, not just someone with a one-time project.

Your Writing Career is a Business—Treat It Like One

Many authors hesitate to embrace the idea that they are a brand and a business. But if you want longevity in your career, you need to approach it with a strategic mindset.

What This Means for You

- **Your Name is Your Brand.** Whether you write fiction or nonfiction, people follow authors, not just books. Think long-term beyond a single title. Keep showing up to be visible.

- **Invest in Professionalism.** A solid author website (even one page), a polished social media presence, and an email list help build credibility.

- **Think Beyond One Book.** What's next? Engage your readers with future projects and keep them invested in your journey. If one book is your goal, remember that connecting and being visible will help you repeatedly attract a new buying audience of readers.

Authors who treat their books and writing like a business create lasting impact. They don't just launch a book; they build a brand.

Create a Plan, Show Up, Stay True to You—Rinse and Repeat

Social media doesn't have to be overwhelming or fake. With a solid plan, an authentic voice, and a commitment to showing up, you can create a powerful online presence that supports both your book and your long-term goals as an author.

If you don't want your story to stop when your book is published, don't stop being visible on social media. Treat it like an extension of your writing career, and watch how it helps you connect with the readers who need your words the most.

Your Author Social Media Toolkit Checklist

Set Your Direction

- Clarify Your Purpose: What's your why behind showing up on social media? (e.g., build community, sell books, share your journey.)
- Pick One Main Goal: What do you want your readers to do? (Join your list? Preorder your book? Engage with your content?)

Know Who You're Talking To

- Define Your Reader Persona: Age, genre preferences, where they spend time online.
- Choose One to Two Platforms: Focus where your ideal reader hangs out. (e.g., YA Fantasy → TikTok and Instagram)

Build a Basic Plan

- Choose Three Pillars of Content: What themes will you post about? (e.g., Behind-the-scenes, Writing Life, Reader Q&A)
- Balance Content Types: Use the 80/20 rule—80 percent engagement, 20 percent promotional.
- Decide on a Posting Rhythm: Three times a week? Weekly check-ins? Set realistic goals you can maintain. Consistency rules the algorithm.

Create with Ease

- Batch Three to Five Posts Ahead of Time: Start small— just get a few ready using tools like Metricool or OneUp.
- Add Visuals: Use Canva to make quote cards, character teasers, or behind-the-scenes graphics.

Show Up Authentically

- Use Your Real Voice: Write captions like you're talking to a friend—because you are.
- Engage Genuinely: Comment back, reply to DMs, and interact with others' posts for just fifteen minutes a day.

Track and Adjust

- Look at What's Working: Use built-in analytics to see what gets likes, shares, or comments, then repeat that style of content.
- Tweak and Try Again: Don't be afraid to experiment. Showing up consistently matters more than being perfect.

Bonus Encouragement Remember that social media isn't meant to be another full-time job. You are a writer/author; that is your job. Give yourself permission to take social media in stride. Little steps can lead to great things. You get to be the boss of your social media bandwidth. You're not behind. You're just getting started. Start messy, stay real, and let your story connect with those who most need it.

SIX

Book Reviews and Endorsements

Deborah Kevin, MA, with Cheri D. Andrews, Esq.

Book reviews and endorsements are critical tools in an author's marketing arsenal, serving as powerful social proof that can significantly influence potential readers' purchasing decisions. Books with a high number of reviews attract more attention and tend to rank higher on platforms like Amazon, increasing their visibility.

According to a study by BookBub, books with over 150 reviews see more than four times increase in sales compared to those with fewer reviews.

Similarly, Goodreads reports that books with more than 1,000 ratings are 97 percent more likely to be included in recommendation lists, further boosting their discoverability. These statistics underscore the importance of actively seeking and promoting reviews and endorsements to enhance your book's credibility and reach.

What are Reviews, Endorsements, and Blurbs?

Book reviews are evaluations of your book written by readers, critics, or bloggers, often posted on platforms like Amazon, Goodreads, or personal blogs. Reviews offer potential readers insights into the book's quality, themes, and appeal, serving as social proof that can influence purchasing decisions.

The quantity and quality of reviews can affect a book's visibility in online stores, as algorithms favor titles with more engagement. Reviews are essential because they provide honest, peer-based evaluations that can attract more readers and build trust in your work.

Endorsements, often called "blurbs," are positive statements about your book typically provided by established authors, experts, or celebrities in your genre. These endorsements are usually found on the book's cover or the front pages. Endorsements lend credibility and prestige to your book, as readers often trust recommendations from recognized figures. A strong endorsement can significantly impact a reader's decision to purchase a book, particularly if the endorser is well-respected.

Advanced reader blurbs are similar to endorsements but are specifically given by early readers, such as those who receive an Advance Reader Copy (ARC) before the book's official release. These blurbs can be used in marketing materials, the book's cover, or online descriptions. Advanced reader blurbs are crucial because they create early buzz around your book and can generate initial reviews even before the book is officially launched.

Book endorsements and advance blurbs are both forms of promotional praise for a book, but they serve distinct purposes and are used at different stages of a book's release.

Book Endorsements. These are typically provided by well-known authors, experts, or industry figures after reading a completed version of the book. Endorsements are often featured on the book's cover or in marketing materials to lend credibility and draw attention, as the endorsers' established reputation can influence readers' decisions.

Advance Blurbs. These are short, positive quotes provided by early readers, such as those who receive an Advance Reader Copy (ARC) of the book before its official release. Blurbs are often used in pre-launch marketing, like promotional emails or social media, to build anticipation and generate buzz around the book.

In summary, endorsements come from respected figures to add authority and credibility, while advance blurbs come from early readers to create excitement and momentum leading up to the book's launch.

While reviews are generally more detailed and come from a broad audience, endorsements, and blurbs are typically shorter and come from specific, often influential, individuals. Reviews provide a wide range of opinions that help other readers gauge the book's general reception. Endorsements offer targeted, high-impact praise that can lend your book instant credibility. Advanced reader blurbs combine the benefits of both, offering early validation that can drive pre-orders and initial sales.

These elements work together to create a robust marketing strategy. Reviews offer a broad base of social proof, endorsements provide authoritative credibility, and advanced reader blurbs generate early excitement and buzz, all contributing to your book's overall success and visibility.

Reviews and Testimonials: The Truth Matters

Your book reviews and endorsements can help make or break the success of your book, but they come with their own set of rules. The Federal Trade Commission (FTC) is cracking down on businesses that manipulate reviews or mislead customers with fake testimonials. The FTC Reviews and Testimonials Rule prohibits six categories of behavior that the FTC deems deceptive:

1. **Fake or False Reviews.** The primary focus of the rule is a strict prohibition on fake or false consumer reviews and testimonials. This covers reviews that misrepresent the reviewer's identity—including those generated by artificial intelligence (AI)—or falsely claim to reflect the experiences of real consumers. This also

applies to testimonials obtained from insiders or purchased from third parties. Under this new regulation, the FTC has made it clear that businesses (yes, as an author, you are in business!) are barred from creating, purchasing, selling, or disseminating such reviews.

2. **Incentivized Reviews.** The FTC's rule also addresses the issue of reviews based on free merchandise, services, or other compensation. The free stuff must be offered without any condition as to the content of the review—positive or negative.

3. **Insider Reviews and Testimonials.** The rule imposes strict limits on reviews and testimonials from company insiders. Any material connection between a reviewer and a business must be clearly and conspicuously disclosed.

4. **Company-Controlled Review Websites.** Another significant aspect of the rule is the prohibition against businesses misrepresenting the independence of review websites or entities they control. Basically, if the company controls the site, they can't claim that the reviews or opinions are impartial.

5. **Fake Social Media Indicators.** The rule also addresses the use of fake social media indicators, such as number of followers or views which are artificially generated through bots or hijacked accounts. It prohibits businesses from inflating their social media influence and deceiving consumers about their popularity or credibility for a commercial purpose. The FTC's regulation prohibits the purchase or sale of such indicators when the buyer knew or should have known that they were fake.

6. **Review Suppression.** Finally, the rule prohibits the suppression of reviews that contain negative or unfavorable content. The rule provides that organizing reviews alone does not qualify as suppressing reviews. Still, businesses **may not feature or highlight favorable reviews in a way that distorts the full universe of consumer feedback**. The rule does not prohibit suppression of reviews that contain defamatory, harassing, abusive, obscene, vulgar or sexually explicit content. Businesses may also suppress clearly false content or reviews that the seller reasonably believes are fake.

To maintain compliance, don't post fake reviews or pay for positive ones, disclose relationships if you feature a review from someone who received a free product, discount, or other compensation, and avoid cherry-picking only your glowing reviews while hiding your negative ones. Bottom line: Be transparent!

Getting Endorsements and Advance Reader Blurbs

The advance reader (ARC) process to obtain blurbs happens after your book has been completely edited and laid out but before proofreading (typically, these happen concurrently).

Typically, your publisher will manage the book blurb process, but you also have a role in finding ARC readers within your community. You'll first ask permission, then either follow these steps yourself or provide your publisher with names and email addresses so she can contact them directly.

1. Reach out via email (or FB messenger or Instagram direct message) to inquire about their interest and availability to read and review your book. Include the following:

- Your book summary (a short paragraph describing your book)

- The total number of pages you're asking them to read (could be the full manuscript or an excerpt)
- What date you need their review by
- Tell them how you'll use their review (back cover copy, interior "Advanced Praise" section, and in marketing copy)

2. When someone says "yes," celebrate! Then follow up by sending them the following information via email (gently remind them that you're not looking for editing or proofreading comments):

- Your manuscript or excerpt (PDF only)
- How you want them to send you the review (email, FB messenger, text)
- What date you need their review by
- Ask if they would also be willing to post a review on Amazon once your book goes live. They should use the following language, "I received an Advanced Reader Copy of the book from the author, and this review is my opinion of said book."

3. If someone says "no," celebrate! Their refusal has nothing to do with you—be grateful they closed the loop.

4. Thank your potential reviewers and those who provided a blurb. Consider offering a free copy of your print or ebook as a concrete way of saying, "Thank you for taking the time to read my book and offer a blurb."

Why Reviews Matter

Book reviews are critical for your book's success. They provide social proof to potential readers and play a key role in boosting your book's visibility on platforms like Amazon and Goodreads. The more reviews you have, the more likely your book will appear in search results, recommendations, and promotions, leading to increased sales and readership.

Book reviews play a crucial role in the longevity and success of a book. Statistics show that books with a higher number of reviews not only gain more visibility but also have a longer sales lifespan. For instance, books with more than 150 reviews significantly increase sales compared to those with fewer reviews, often boosting sales by up to 4.5 times[4]. This increased visibility is due to algorithms on platforms like Amazon, which favor books with more reviews, pushing them higher in search results and recommendations[5].

Moreover, the average book sells around 200 copies in its first year, but this number can rise significantly with a strong review presence, potentially reaching 1,000 copies over its lifetime. This demonstrates that actively seeking and accumulating reviews can significantly extend a book's market presence and enhance its long-term success.

Securing reviews is not just about initial sales but about sustaining your book's relevance and visibility in a competitive market over time.

Where to Get Reviews

- **Amazon:** The most influential platform for reviews. Reviews here directly impact your book's ranking and visibility.

- **Goodreads:** A hub for book lovers, where reviews can help build credibility and connect with a community of readers. https://www.goodreads.com/

- **StoryGraph:** This is an excellent non-Amazon alternative to Goodreads. https://www.thestorygraph.com/

- **LibraryThing:** An engaged group of readers, who enter a lottery to win the chance to read and review your book. If they win, they are obligated to provide a review on LibraryThing. As the author, you determine how many of your books to include in the giveaway, and your publisher sets it up within LibraryThing. This is a fantastic way to interact with potential fans—you can include a thank you note and flat SWAG with your book to readers. https://www.librarything.com/

- **Book Blogs**: Reach out to bloggers who specialize in your genre. A positive review from a well-regarded blog can drive significant interest.

- **Social Media:** Encourage readers to share their thoughts on platforms like Instagram, Twitter, and Facebook, where their networks can see their recommendations. Be sure to ask them to tag you so you can see (and share) their reviews.

- **Book Clubs and Reader Communities:** Engage with book clubs and online reading communities. These groups often post reviews and discuss books in detail.

How Often to Ask for Reviews

- **Immediately After Purchase:** Prompt readers to leave a review shortly after they purchase or finish your book. This is when the experience is freshest in their minds.

- **During Promotional Campaigns:** If you're running a discount or giveaway, ask readers to leave a review in exchange for a free or discounted copy.

- **Post-Event:** Remind attendees to leave a review after virtual or in-person events like book signings or readings.

- **Regularly on Social Media:** Periodically remind your followers to leave a review, especially when you hit milestones (like 100 reviews).

- **Ongoing in Your Newsletter:** Include a review link to one review site in every email, reminding readers how crucial their reviews are.

How to Ask for Reviews

When asking for reviews, being polite, clear, and respectful of your readers' time is important. Here are some tips:

- **Be Direct, But Not Pushy:** Make it clear that reviews are valuable to you but avoid making the reader feel pressured.

- **Personalize Your Request**: If you're emailing or messaging individual readers, personalize your request to show you value their opinion.

- **Provide Easy Instructions:** Include direct links to where they can leave a review to make the process as simple as possible.

- **Express Gratitude**: Always thank your readers for their support, whether or not they choose to leave a review.

Email Script for Requesting Reviews

Here's a simple, effective email script you can use to ask for reviews:

Subject: A Quick Favor for [Your Book Title]

Hi [Reader's Name],

I hope this message finds you well! I wanted to take a moment to thank you for reading [Your Book Title]. It means the world to me that you took the time to dive into my work.

If you enjoyed the book, I would be incredibly grateful if you could take a few minutes to leave a review on [Amazon/Goodreads/Other Platform]. Your feedback not only helps other readers discover the book but also supports my journey as an author. Here's the link to leave your review: [Insert Link].

Thank you so much for your support—I truly appreciate it!

Best wishes,
[Your Name]

Tips for Reviewers

As a believer in karma, I feel that one must write and publish reviews to receive them. Follow these tips to write effective and helpful reviews for the books you read. You can also incorporate these tips into your email requesting reviews.

- Don't be fancy—write in short, easy-to-read sentences.
- Start with facts about the book—offer review readers clarity on what you'll cover.
- Avoid spoilers (or alert readers for potential spoilers).
- Offer comparisons (e.g., If you enjoyed X, you'll enjoy Y).
- Say what you loved and what you wanted that wasn't there.
- Put yourself in other readers' shoes: What would you have wanted to know before you picked up this book?

Additional Tips for Gathering Reviews

- **Follow-up:** If someone mentioned they enjoyed your book but has yet to leave a review, follow up with a gentle reminder.

Pro Tip: If someone tells you how much they enjoyed your book, jot down their verbal review, write it up, and send it to them with a note that you hope it's okay that you drafted a review for them to post. Tell them to feel free to edit the review before posting.

- **Offer Incentives:** While you can't directly offer rewards for reviews on platforms like Amazon, you can offer incentives like entry into a giveaway for those who post honest reviews.

- **Engage with Reviewers:** Thank reviewers personally and engage with them on social media. This builds a relationship and encourages future reviews.

By strategically asking for reviews and making the process as easy as possible for your readers, you can significantly increase the number of reviews for your book, boosting its visibility and success.

How to Use Book Reviews

Book reviews are more than just feedback from readers; they are powerful tools that can be strategically leveraged to enhance your book's visibility, credibility, and sales. Whether you're a new author or a seasoned writer, knowing how to effectively use reviews can make a significant difference in your marketing efforts. This section explores various ways to utilize book reviews to maximize their impact, from boosting your online presence to incorporating them into your promotional materials.

Highlight Reviews on Your Website

- **Why It Matters**: Featuring positive reviews on your website adds credibility and can persuade potential readers to purchase your book. Create a dedicated section for testimonials or feature quotes on your homepage to showcase the praise your book has received.

- **How to Do It**: Select the most impactful excerpts from reviews and display them prominently on your site. Include the reviewer's name and source if possible to enhance authenticity.

Use Reviews in Social Media Marketing

- **Why It Matters**: Social media platforms are excellent for sharing book reviews with a wider audience. Posting excerpts from reviews can generate interest and encourage your followers to check out your book.

- **How to Do It**: Share snippets of glowing reviews on platforms like Instagram, Twitter, and Facebook. Accompany the quotes with a call to action, such as a link to purchase the book or a prompt to leave their own review.

Pro Tip: Using Canva, create a "testimonial" template, duplicate, update the reviews, and download. Save all the testimonial images to a digital file to be used as part of your overall social media strategy.

Incorporate Reviews into Your Book's Description

- **Why It Matters**: Including reviews in your book's product description on sites like Amazon or Goodreads can immediately provide potential buyers with social proof of your book's quality.

- **How to Do It**: Add a few standout quotes from professional reviewers or enthusiastic readers to the top of your book's description. Ensure these reviews are concise and impactful, highlighting key aspects of your book that appeal to readers. Your publisher ought to do this when uploading your book files to the various publishing sites.

Leverage Reviews in Email Campaigns

- **Why It Matters**: Email marketing is a direct way to reach potential readers and including positive reviews can increase engagement and conversion rates.

- **How to Do It**: When sending newsletters or promotional emails, include a short review snippet alongside information about your book. This builds interest and provides social proof that can encourage purchases.

Include Reviews in Print Materials

- **Why It Matters**: Reviews can also be effectively used in physical marketing materials like bookmarks, postcards, or flyers, especially during book launches or signings.

- **How to Do It**: Print excerpts of the best reviews on promotional materials you distribute at events or include with purchases. This tangible endorsement can reinforce your book's appeal.

Pitch Media Outlets Using Reviews

- **Why It Matters**: When reaching out to media outlets, bloggers, or influencers for additional coverage, including positive reviews can strengthen your pitch and increase the likelihood of being featured.

- **How to Do It**: Attach a press kit with a summary of the best reviews and your pitch. Highlighting strong reviews can help convince media contacts that your book is worth their attention.

Use Reviews in Advertising

- **Why It Matters**: Advertisements featuring compelling reviews can enhance the credibility of your book and increase click-through rates.

- **How to Do It**: Incorporate short, positive quotes from reviews into your online ads, such as Facebook or Google Ads. Highlighting a reviewer's praise in your ad copy can draw attention and persuade potential readers to learn more.

Note: Paid advertising can be a waste of marketing resources. People discover books through various channels, with some being more influential than others.

According to a Penguin Random House study, word of mouth remains the most powerful method, influencing around 49 percent of readers' decisions. Online retailers like Amazon are also significant, with around 26 percent of readers discovering books this way. Social media is increasingly important, especially among younger demographics, impacting about 20 percent of readers. Book reviews and recommendations from trusted sources also play a key role in guiding readers' choices.

You'll notice that "paid advertising" is not a top way for people to discover your books.

By strategically using book reviews across various platforms and marketing channels, you can amplify their impact, enhancing your book's reputation and driving sales. Reviews serve as powerful endorsements that, when used effectively, can help you reach a broader audience and build lasting success.

How to Get Book Reviews from Publications

- Send out review copies of your book. Lots of them. More than you think you ought to.
- Send ARCs and your EPK to every major newspaper and magazine that might be interested in your book's subject.
- For every 100 copies you send out, you get 200 orders—a pretty great return on investment (ROI).
- Budget 5-10 percent of your first printing as giveaways —for reviewers, booksellers, and key opinion makers.

Here is a list of potential nonfiction book reviewers to whom you could send an advanced reader copy (ARC) or your book after publication, along with your electronic press kit. Note: Read and follow each publication's submission guidelines. Some require paperback copies, others take PDF copies, and others want ebook copies.

- ***Publishers Weekly***: http://www.bookmarket.com/pw.html.
- ***Kirkus Reviews***: Sarah Gold (nonfiction), 200 Park Avenue South #1118, New York, NY 10003-1543.
- ***Booklist***: Mary Ellen Quinn, Booklist, American Library Association, 50 E. Huron St., Chicago, IL 60611-2729 or www.ala.org/booklist (two copies needed).
- ***Choice***: Book Review Editor, *Choice*, 100 Riverview Center, Middletown, CT 06457 OR email submissions@ala-choice.org (they review finished books only).
- ***Washington Post Book World***: Nina King, Editor, *Washington Post Book World*, 1150 15th Street NW, Washington, DC 20071 (http://www.washingtonpost.com).
- ***San Francisco Chronicle Book Review***: Patricia Holt, Review Editor, *San Francisco Chronicle*, 275 Fifth Street, San Francisco, CA 94103 OR email: patholt@sfgate.com.
- ***Los Angeles Times Book Review***: Steve Wasserman, Book Review Editor, *Los Angeles Times Book Review*, Times Mirror Square, Los Angeles, CA 90053.
- ***Chicago Tribune Books***: Elizabeth Taylor, Book Review Editor, *Chicago Tribune Books*, 435 N. Michigan Avenue, Room 400, Chicago, IL 66011-4022.
- ***USA Today***: Deirdre Donohue, Book Review Editor, *USA Today*, 1000 Wilson Blvd., Arlington, VA 22229.
- ***New York Review of Books***: Robert B. Silvers or Barbara Epstein, Editors, *New York Review of Books*, 1755 Broadway, 5th Floor, New York, NY 10019.
- ***Midwest Book Review***: James Cox, Midwest Book Review, 278 Orchard Drive, Oregon, Wisconsin 53575.

SEVEN

Email Marketing and Newsletters

Deborah Kevin, MA, with Cheri D. Andrews, Esq.

Email marketing and newsletters are crucial for authors to build and maintain direct relationships with their readers. Unlike social media, which is often subject to algorithm changes, email provides a reliable, personal way to communicate directly with your audience. Newsletters allow you to share updates, exclusive content, and promotional offers, keeping your readers engaged and informed about your work. This consistent interaction strengthens reader loyalty, drives book sales, and supports long-term career growth by fostering a dedicated, engaged community.

Email marketing and newsletters are closely related but serve different purposes in an author's promotional strategy.

- **Email Marketing:** A broader strategy that encompasses all types of email communications sent to your audience, including promotional offers, sales announcements, event invitations, and updates about your books. Its primary goal is to drive specific actions, like purchasing a book or signing up for an event.

- **Newsletters:** A specific type of email content focused on providing regular, curated updates to your subscribers. Newsletters often include a mix of personal updates, upcoming events, exclusive content, and links to recent blog posts or media appearances. The goal is to build relationships with your readers and keep them engaged over time.

While email marketing is often more transactional, newsletters are relationship-building tools, fostering ongoing engagement with your audience.

Email marketing and newsletters are potent tools for authors to build strong, lasting connections with their readers. You can keep your readers engaged and informed by consistently delivering valuable content, updates, and exclusive offers directly to your audience's inbox. Whether announcing a new release, sharing behind-the-scenes insights, or offering special promotions, email is a personal and effective way to nurture your reader community. By planning your content, utilizing the right software, and maintaining a regular schedule, you can maximize the impact of your email marketing and newsletters, ultimately driving your success as an author.

Email and the CAN-SPAM Act

In the United States, email marketing is governed by the CAN-SPAM Act, which the Federal Trade Commission enforces. The act applies to commercial email (selling) in nature, including any email designed to promote the sale of your book. Transactional email (facilitating a transaction the customer has already agreed to) is exempt, but the act will apply if an email contains both commercial and transactional material. When in doubt, make sure your email is compliant. Each individual email that violates the act is subject to fines in excess of $51,000; therefore, failure to comply can be costly.

To be compliant with the CAN-SPAM Act, all your book marketing emails should follow the following seven requirements:

1. **Don't use false or misleading header information**. The "From," "To," "Reply-To," and routing information must accurately identify the person or business who initiated the message.

2. **Don't use deceptive subject lines**. The subject line must accurately reflect the content of the message. Don't use cute or clever "click-bait" titles unless the content actually covers that title.

3. **Admit that it's advertising**. Disclose clearly and conspicuously that your message is an advertisement. There is no magic formula for this—it can be as simple as text at the bottom of the email stating, "This advertisement was sent by (your business name here)."

4. **Provide a valid physical address**. A physical address must be included on every email. This can be your street address, a post office box, or a private mailbox registered with a commercial agency. Basically, any address where physical mail can be received.

5. **Provide an opt-out mechanism**. Your email must include a clear and simple way for the recipient to opt out of your email list.

6. **Handle opt-out requests promptly**. You must honor an opt-out request within ten business days. The Act also prohibits selling or transferring any email address that has opted out, so make sure they are removed from your database.

7. **Monitor work done on your behalf**. If you're working with a marketing agency or a platform like Mailchimp, don't assume compliance. The responsibility ultimately falls on *you*. Double-check your campaigns

before hitting "send." Both your company and the
company actually sending the message may be held
legally responsible for any violation of the CAN-
SPAM Act.

Email Marketing

Email marketing is vital for authors to engage with their readers and
promote their work directly. This format is ideal for:

- Announcing new book releases
- Offering exclusive discounts
- Promoting upcoming events
- Sharing limited-time deals
- Special announcements like pre-orders
- Early access to new content

Best practices suggest sending marketing emails sparingly—typically no more than once or twice a month—to avoid overwhelming
your subscribers while keeping them engaged and informed. Consistency, value-driven content, and clear calls to action are key to
successful email marketing for authors.

Can Email Marketing Items Be Added to a Newsletter?

Whether to include book or event announcements in a newsletter or
keep them separate depends on your audience and the content's
frequency. If your newsletter already includes diverse content and
your announcements fit naturally, it can be effective to combine
them. This keeps your readers informed without overwhelming
them with multiple emails. However, for significant announcements
like a new book release or a major event, sending a dedicated email
can help ensure the message stands out and receives the attention it
deserves. Balancing these approaches is key to maintaining engagement without causing email fatigue.

How Long Should a Marketing Email Be?

An email marketing email should be concise and focused, typically between fifty and 200 words. The key is to convey your message clearly without overwhelming the reader. This length allows you to include essential details, such as a brief announcement, a call to action, and any necessary links, while maintaining the reader's attention. Keep your email skimmable with short paragraphs, bullet points, or **bold text** for emphasis, ensuring that the main message is easily grasped at a glance.

Best Practices for Email Graphics

- **Keep It Simple**: Use clean, minimalistic designs that don't overwhelm the reader. Graphics should enhance, not overshadow, your message.

- **Optimize for Mobile**: Ensure graphics are responsive and look good on all devices. Mobile accounts for a significant portion of email opens.

- **Maintain Brand Consistency**: Use your brand's colors, fonts, and style in graphics to reinforce brand identity.

- **Include Alt Text**: Add descriptive alt text to graphics in case the images don't load.

- **Use Eye-Catching Images**: Choose high-quality visuals that draw attention and align with your content. DO NOT use images off the internet, as you could get into copyright troubles. Ensure that you have the appropriate licenses for use.

- **Limit File Size**: Keep images optimized for faster loading times without sacrificing quality.

- **Call to Action (CTA)**: Incorporate clear, clickable CTAs within your graphics, guiding readers on the next steps.

Newsletters

Author newsletters are a tool for building and maintaining a direct connection with your readers. Newsletters allow you to share updates, personal insights, exclusive content, and upcoming releases in a personalized way. Consistency is key to keeping your audience engaged; regular newsletters, whether weekly, monthly, or quarterly, ensure your readers remain interested in your journey. By providing valuable and timely content, you create a loyal readership that eagerly anticipates each update, ultimately driving deeper engagement and long-term success as an author. The key to consistently creating and publishing an impactful newsletter is following the KISS principle—keep it simple, silly! I suggest publishing your newsletter monthly on the same day of the month (for example, the first Sunday or the third Wednesday).

Five cardinal rules for writing and publishing your newsletter:

1. Be consistent. Once you've established a rhythm with once a month, you can expand to twice a month or weekly.
2. Keep it simple and brief.
3. Include photos of your writing space, work-in-progress, garden, vacation, hobbies, bookshelves, and pets— especially your pets!
4. Show your personality—readers want to know YOU much more than they want to know your books.
5. Have FUN!

Here are additional ideas to include in your monthly author newsletter that incorporate photos:

- **Behind-the-scenes**: Share images of your writing space, inspiration boards, or drafts in progress.

- **Character or Setting Visuals**: Showcase images that represent characters or settings from your book.

- **Bookstagram Style**: Feature aesthetically arranged photos of your books, including fan-submitted shots.

- **Author Life:** Include personal snapshots, such as attending events, speaking engagements, or traveling.

- **Exclusive Excerpts:** Pair a photo with a snippet from your upcoming book.

- **Fan Art or Reader Photos**: Share visuals from readers engaging with your book.

Newsletter Layout

Here's a simple newsletter layout that balances personal connection and event updates while highlighting your personality:

[Your Name's] Monthly Musings

Letter from the Author
A friendly, conversational note about your writing process, recent life events, or inspiration. (Insert a candid or relatable photo of yourself.)

Upcoming Events (or Publications)

[Event Name]: Date and time with a brief description.
[Event Name]: Date and time with RSVP or registration link. (Include event-related images or promotional banners.)

This Month's Highlight
A quirky, fun section showcasing something personal, like favorite books, writing tools, or a favorite hobby. (Add a playful or themed image.)

In the News
Highlight a review or something bookish that's grabbing the world by storm. You can also share your own reviews of other authors' work.

This layout is approachable and engaging and lets your personality shine through!

Planning and Leveraging Your Newsletter

Planning your author newsletter and social media content can ease the burden of consistency and provide valuable content to your readers. By organizing your themes in advance, you can ensure a steady flow of engaging updates without feeling rushed or overwhelmed. Each month can focus on a different aspect of your author journey or content that resonates with your audience.

Authors don't need to create all content from scratch; sharing information from other authors or publications can enrich newsletters and social media posts. Curating content like writing tips, book recommendations, or industry insights provides value and supports fellow writers.

For example, an author can share an insightful article on character development or recommend a book that influenced their writing style. This practice fosters a sense of community, saves time, and keeps content fresh. Associating with respected sources adds credibility to your platform. Always, always, always cite the author and publication!

Monthly Newsletter Theme Examples

- **January**: New Year reflections and writing goals
- **February**: Behind-the-scenes of your writing process

- **March**: Book recommendations or influences
- **April**: Upcoming releases and teasers
- **May**: Q&A session with readers
- **June**: Favorite writing tools or tips
- **July**: Summer reading lists
- **August**: Character or setting spotlights
- **September**: Exclusive content, like short stories or excerpts
- **October**: Book club or reader group discussions
- **November**: Gratitude-themed updates or promotions
- **December**: Year-in-review and holiday greetings

You can also use the National Day and International Day calendars (https://www.nationaldaycalendar.com/ and https://www.nationaldaycalendar.com/international) for your newsletter and social media posts.

This planned approach keeps your readers engaged and eagerly anticipating each newsletter, building loyalty and driving your long-term success. It also makes your life much easier!

Email Newsletter Software

Choosing the right email marking and newsletter software is essential. The following are some popular tools that offer user-friendly interfaces and powerful features for authors:

- **Mailchimp**: Known for its ease of use and free tier, Mailchimp offers customizable templates, analytics, and audience segmentation, making it perfect for beginners and small mailing lists. To pre-schedule emails and newsletters for release, which I highly recommend, you'll need to purchase the inexpensive paid version. https://mailchimp.com/

- **MailerLite:** Offers simplicity and affordability with drag-and-drop editors, automation, and built-in surveys, perfect for authors who want streamlined features at a low cost. https://www.mailerlite.com/

- **ActiveCampaign:** A robust platform with advanced automation, personalization, and detailed reporting. Ideal for authors looking to scale their email marketing efforts. https://www.activecampaign.com/

Keep things simple. Start with an easy-to-use software and re-evaluate your needs annually. Most email software systems allow you to easily upload your existing email list from one platform to another.

EIGHT

Promotional Materials

Suzanne Tregenza

Promotional materials are critical to consistently spreading the word about your book. This chapter shares all the materials you'll want to consider throughout the book's life cycle.

Usually, I begin working with authors before their book launches and often continue until long after completion. Let's take this in order. Try not to get overwhelmed; you don't need everything all at once.

Get Quality Images

The best advice I can give is to request a selection of quality images of your book's cover from the graphic designer who created it. You will use these throughout the book's life cycle and having them handy will help make all my following recommendations easier.

I love to have the following on hand when working with a client:

- The flat front cover of the book
- Three-dimensional images leaning both right and left
- A three-dimensional image of the flat front cover

- Images that show the book cover on cell phones, tablets, and a computer screen
- An image that shows the cover on multiple devices together
- The cover adjusted for use on an audiobook
- The audiobook cover with a set of headphones

Be certain to request JPGs, PNGs, and .AI files for each of the above and tuck them away somewhere safe. Once you have your basic graphics in hand, everything else becomes easier.

Sharing Your Book Graphics on Social Media

Prior to your book launch, you'll likely promote your book without graphics until you do an official cover reveal. No doubt you will get some great in-depth advice about this in the social media chapter of this book, but four must-do promotions for your social media and your email marketing are:

- **Guess what? I'm writing a book!** In this post, you will want to share what you are writing, a working title, and why you are writing it;

- **Cover reveal.** This post will be the first time you share your final book cover with your audience;

- **Launch date announcement.** Let your raving fans know when your book will become available and what kind of incentive you might have for purchasing on launch day; and,

- **Today is the day!** Mark the occasion of your launch with the full-court press of promotion so that no one in your sphere can miss the launch of your book.

For most of these, you will want to include an appropriately sized graphic for the application.

Press Releases

In addition to sharing the news of your book with your social media and email marketing communities, you'll want to share it with the world. The best way to do this is to craft and distribute a press release, depending on the pitch angles you will take.

At the basic level, you will want a release that announces the book's availability, you as the author, who the book is for, and what problems it solves. If the book aligns directly with your business, you will likely wish to include a description of your business and offerings to which the book might lead people.

You may consider additional press releases targeting more specific audiences: perhaps one highlighting you as a local author distributed to your local media outlets or one to trade publications to highlight your leadership in your field. Once you have a basic release, altering it for a narrower audience can be a snap.

Preparing for Your Book Launch

The launch is the beginning of the book's life cycle. When working with clients to launch their books, I create two sets of promotional materials: the graphics and the written materials.

Graphics That Speak for You

Graphics generally include images of the book and/or the author. Some are simple and have just a book cover. Others include quotes from the book, or promotional blurbs collected by advance readers of the manuscript. All contain a direct, simple URL to a page where the book can be purchased. For my clients I typically create between four and ten graphics.

Written Materials for Your Launch Partners

Because I lead clients through a launch with promotional partners, I also create written materials for their launch partners. These include:

- **Social media posts.** Geared for the platforms most likely used by the author and her community. Most posts are between fifteen and fifty words and include a direct call to action for immediate book purchase.

- **Email subject lines.** Crafted to simply get the email opened. A few compelling words aimed at the book's target audience can make all the difference—because unopened emails don't sell books.

- **Promotional email copy.** Typically, 150–200 words. It introduces the author and the book, shares compelling marketing copy about who the book is for and what problems it solves, and includes a strong call to action in both the body and postscript.

Ongoing Promotional Phase

After your book launch, you still need promotional materials similar to those already identified but updated to remove the urgency created for the launch. You are now in the ongoing promotional phase.

Refresh Your Graphics

Update launch graphics to reflect the book's continued availability and accolades:

- Replace "NEW BOOK! AVAILABLE NOW!" with "AVAILABLE ON AMAZON" or similar.

- Add bestseller or "best new release" status with specific rankings and categories.
- Continue using quotes and blurbs from advanced readers.
- Expand your library with star ratings and reviews from Amazon or other platforms.

Revise Your Written Materials

Your audience and message haven't changed, but your messaging should reflect the shift away from launch-day urgency:

- Pull in snippets from your book to keep your content relevant.
- Incorporate quotes or themes from the book into email copy, newsletters, or blogs.
- Keep promoting the same transformation your book offers—just without the time-sensitive framing.

Create a Book Trailer

A short video book trailer can be made at any time and used widely:

- Use copy and imagery from your existing materials.
- Post it on your website, social media, presentations, and Amazon book page.

Don't Hide Your Authorship

Many authors forget to update existing assets to include their book. Once you're an author, everyone should know it:

- Include your book in your bio on your business website, social media accounts, speaker one-sheets.
- Even if you don't use the full author bio you crafted from

guidance in Chapter 2, be sure that some version includes your authorship.
- Add your book to your email signature.
- Mention it in your speaker bios and presentation decks.

Leverage Passive Promotions

Let your book promote itself quietly and continuously:

- Use social media banners with your book's image and key details.
- Keep one as your default banner, so it's always working in the background.

Mail Flat SWAG

Flat SWAG is one of the most effective (and fun!) ongoing promotional tools. Fun Fact: SWAG stands for Stuff We All Get. These easy-to-mail items include:

- Bookmarks
- Stickers
- Bookplates

Use them to:

- Incentivize purchases on launch day.
- Thank your promotional partners.
- Hand out at events for low-cost, high-impact marketing.

Pro tip: Make sure every item includes your website URL.

Invest in a Banner Stand for Speaking Gigs

If you speak in person, a banner stand is a must-have:

- Feature your book cover prominently—large enough to read from across the room.
- Use it at talks, book signings, and vendor tables to sell books and build visibility.

Your Book's Journey Continues

There may come a time where you write your next book in your evolution. Especially if your initial book reached a bestseller ranking, be sure that is noted on the cover of your subsequent books. Writing a new book is a fantastic way to sell a previously published one.

I would be remiss if I didn't mention developing a media kit to include in your promotional materials. This piece is so important, you'll read more about why and how to create one in Chapter 9.

As I mentioned at the beginning of this chapter, creating all the promotional materials listed can feel like eating an elephant. Starting with a great set of book graphics will make it easier, then chip away at the rest of the list. You can do this. I believe in you.

Growing Your Audience

NINE

Leveraging Media

Suzanne Tregenza

If you're serious about growing your author brand, it's time to think beyond the bookshelf. Media exposure—whether through podcasts, interviews, guest appearances, or panels—is one of the most powerful tools you have to expand your reach, deepen your credibility, and spark meaningful connections with your ideal audience. Visibility in the media doesn't just boost book sales; it builds trust, positions you as an expert, and opens doors to unexpected opportunities. The good news? You don't need to be famous or have a publicist to get booked—you just need to be prepared. In this chapter, we'll walk you through how to build a standout media kit and share insider tips for landing and leveraging interviews that align with your message and mission.

What Is a Media Kit?

A professional media kit is one of the most beneficial items for book promotion. Having one that is well-crafted and easy to provide has enabled me to participate in many interviews and speaking events that otherwise would have been a chore. It may take a little while to put together, but having it will save you time in applying for and following up on speaking and interview opportunities forever after.

What To Include in Your Media Kit

First, I'll discuss what you want in your media kit and why. Then, I'll share what I believe are the best formats for both owner-friendly and user-friendly media kits. The elements you'll want in your media kit are as follows:

- Headshots
- Author bio
- Book image(s)
- Book summary
- Book metadata
- Advanced reader blurbs
- Social media links
- Other publications
- Other media appearances
- Frequently asked questions
- Media contact information

Headshots

Headshots are often the first visual impression event hosts get of you. Offering a range of professional shots helps you fit into various promotional materials, from social media posts to event banners. Almost anyone booking you to speak to their audience will want a headshot to promote the event. Make this easy for them and include a few options so they can select what fits their style best.

Author Bio

You must be introduced to the audience you are connecting with. Having a variety of bios of different lengths prepared is extremely helpful. Short bios are typically needed for introductions, while a longer bio can provide more context for event programs or marketing. Be sure to have a simple, approximately seventy-five-word bio. I have also been asked for a 150-character bio, so be prepared to cut yours to bare bones if necessary. (Revisit Chapter 2 for support in writing compelling author bios.)

Book Image(s)

Your host or event leader may want to include these in promotional materials if you are specifically speaking about your book.

Book Summary

You likely put considerable time and energy into the marketing copy on your book jacket. You can leverage the description from the back of your book for your media kit. Event promoters will likely use this content, and interviewers will certainly use it to get a sense of what your book is about and why it may be appropriate for their audience.

Book Metadata

Please include the title, publisher (if applicable), publication date, published formats, your website, and, if available, the location where it can be purchased.

Advance Reader Blurbs

If you have pre-reader promotional blurbs or reviews worth sharing, include some of the best in your media kit.

Social Media Links

Make it easy for hosts and potential hosts to check you out and connect with you on your social media accounts. Don't just put the handle; put an active link that opens right to your account. Also, remember that consistency with your social media matters. It reinforces credibility and will show potential hosts or interviewers you regularly engage with your followers. This will have a positive impact on their decision-making process.

Other Publications

Every publication you've participated in increases your credibility. If there are a few, include them all. If there are many, include the most prominent and most recent. Keep in mind: If you've contributed guest posts or been featured in prominent publications, including these publications, your authority will also be elevated.

Other Media Appearances

Provide links to what you feel are your best prior interviews or speaking engagements. If you have several of these, provide a variety, including podcasts, interviews, and live talks to appeal to a broader range of hosts. If you don't already have these, keep them in mind as you develop and grow.

Frequently Asked Questions (FAQs)

By providing a list of questions an interviewer or panel leader may ask you and the answers, they can expect to get aid in the decision-making process of whether to grant you an interview or speaking opportunity. Providing anticipated questions and answers also ensures you are prepared and can steer the discussion toward your key messages.

Media Contact Information

A media contact can simply be your name, email, and phone number. However, a friend of mine always uses a fake name with his information because that way, if he answers a call and the person asks for the fake name, he knows it is a media inquiry and can prioritize it. This proactive strategy makes recognizing media inquiries easy and responding swiftly, which is crucial for capitalizing on opportunities.

Optional Items

While not essential, these next elements can significantly enhance your media kit's effectiveness—especially if you're looking to build long-term relationships with your audience. Including a giveaway or "lead magnet" not only provides value to listeners or attendees but also helps you grow your email list—an author's most valuable marketing asset. Pairing your offer with a visual (such as a mock-up or image of the gift) can further increase engagement by giving hosts a tool to promote you and giving potential readers a memorable reason to take action. Think of these extras as high-impact, low-effort ways to extend the reach of every media appearance.

- **Details About Your Launch Giveaway.** Having a gift for each audience you connect with is extremely valuable, as it allows you to collect email addresses for future marketing purposes. I understand you are trying to sell books, but getting leads on your email address may be more important and allow you to reintroduce your book to people who may not have purchased it initially. Your lead magnet isn't just about selling your book. It's about building long-term relationships with your audience, offering them value that encourages further engagement.

- **Gift Image.** An image of your giveaway can help your host promote it and provide participants or listeners with a visual reminder of your offer.

Above, I've described an extremely comprehensive media kit. There may be items you don't yet have. You may question the need for others. I like to think of a media kit as a living document, not something you craft once and put away on a shelf. It will develop as you do, so don't be discouraged if you're lacking. Just begin with what you have and keep building.

Now, let's move on to creating your media kit. Many would tell you that graphically designing your media kit is important. I disagree,, because you are creating a living document. Developing something that will morph over time requires flexibility in its design.

Make Your Media Kit Easily Accessible

As a podcast host, receiving a beautifully designed media kit PDF is often my worst nightmare. If I want to include my guest's bio somewhere, I can't easily lift the text. Instead, I must retype it. Often, I am left without usable headshots and need to request them. And my favorite issue? Guests regularly share that elements of their beautiful media kit are outdated, providing me with new details at the last minute.

So, what is the best alternative to avoid these dilemmas? I recommend building your media kit in a Word document hosted on Dropbox, or a Google Doc hosted on your Google Drive and providing the appropriate link to access it. When you provide your kit this way, you can easily update it, and the user of the materials can copy text from it, avoiding potential typos. This kit should include a link to a folder that houses JPG and PNG files for all the images included in the media kit, thereby preserving the integrity of your files.

This style of media kit also helps you too.. For example, many speaker applications have their own form and format; submitting a media kit does not suffice. When your media kit is in a simple document format, everything you need to fill out an application is available for you to copy and paste. From my experience, this is an invaluable time saver.

Begin With The Basics. Then, Build From There

Please don't be overwhelmed by this process. You may not have everything I've listed here for your media kit–and that's okay! Begin with the basics and continue to build it over time.

Remember that your media kit is a living document. Updating it doesn't have to be overwhelming. Set a reminder to review and refresh it every few months or after significant milestones, such as new publications or speaking events.

Now that you know what should be in your media kit and how it should be crafted begin by pulling together the needed elements and building your kit. You'll never regret the work you put into it, and make it easier on you by starting your media kit today.

Obtaining and Leveraging Interviews

Being interviewed is one of the best ways to promote your book consistently. That's because interviews bring attention to authors. Thanks to the numerous podcasts available, there are significantly more opportunities for interviews. Not only do interviews bring visibility, they position you as an authority in your field, elevating your reputation and attracting new clients and opportunities. I work with clients to help them get booked, get visible, get leads, and get clients through interviews, and I'm excited to share my strategies with you.

First things first, you will need a media kit, which I discussed in the previous section. Media kits are a crucial element in getting booked for interviews. Every host will need your assets, and the media kit will provide them.

Research Before Applying for Interviews

When seeking interview opportunities, be sure that your core messages will resonate with the interviewer's audience. Researching ahead of time will reduce rejection and frustration. Show hosts will not bring you on if it isn't clear that you have something to offer their community. Do your homework on the shows you apply for rather than for every show possible. Here are a few suggestions on how to ensure your message is aligned to their audience:

- Review the host's social media to get a sense of her community. If these are your people, you'll likely be able to tell very quickly.
- Listen to past episodes to understand their tone, format, and topics. This is helpful so that you aren't surprised by questions asked on every episode, and so that you have a sense of the direction the host takes her interviews.
- Check how engaged the audience is. For example, are there listener reviews or social media discussions? If there is feedback, this will also help you get a sense of the host's audience and what engages them.

Start With Newer Shows

As you begin to reach out to show hosts, start with newer podcasts or smaller shows to build your experience and confidence. These hosts are often more eager to feature fresh voices, and as you get better at interviews, you'll be ready to approach bigger, more established shows. It is tempting to want to be interviewed in the largest venue with the widest audience right from the start. However, being interviewed is a skill that takes a while to master. If your early interviews are with new hosts on new shows that don't yet have huge followings, they can still be beneficial, and if you struggle to put your best foot forward, they won't create any disasters. Think of them as practice for future, larger opportunities.

Where to Look for Interviews

If you are unsure where to look for interviews, there are two tried-and-true ways to find shows that will host you.

First, think of one or two people in your industry who you consider to be your mentors. These individuals should have the same or similar area of expertise as you but are likely a bit ahead of you in others' recognition. Do a Google search for their name and podcast, or their name and interview. More than likely, you will receive a list of shows these individuals have been a guest on. This is a great initial list of shows for you to apply to.

For more traditional media interviews, sign up for a free account on SOS Media Inquiries (https://www.sourceofsources.com). Select appropriate keywords and search terms, and you will see reporters seeking to interview those with your expertise. Note that opportunities on SOS come and go quickly, so if you aren't committed to reviewing them at least daily, you may want to focus your energy on booking podcast interviews.

If this seems cumbersome to you, and you are financially able to, hiring a podcast booking agency or a public relations (PR) firm is always an option. Just be ready to invest over time because a PR agency can take a while to gain momentum.

Nail Your Core Messages

Once you've booked an interview, it is important to leverage it effectively. The first way to do this is to be clear on the messages you want to convey to the host's audience. If your media kit is well prepared, you will provide suggested questions to your interviewer. That doesn't mean she will use them. Always be prepared to steer the conversation toward your key messages, even if the host's questions aren't a direct fit. Skilled interviewees know how to guide their answers toward their core messages without sounding off-topic.

This requires a rock-solid understanding of your core messages and experience with interviewing. With each interview, you can better hear a host's question and slide one of your core messages into the answer. If you watch any political news, you likely see interviewees do this all the time. They answer a question with the talking points they wish to get across. Fortunately, your message will likely be much more aligned with your host's questions than the questions and answers often seen in the political news media.

Key Audience Takeaways

Part of leveraging your interview is focusing on the action you want listeners to take and ensuring that action helps you. Your book may be a key part of why you are being interviewed, but remember that those listening don't already know, like, and trust you.

Instead of just focusing on selling your book, offer a valuable resource, like a free eBook or a checklist, that aligns with the interview topic. This will help you build a relationship with the listener and keep them engaged after the interview.

While I know you want to sell books, what you want more than anything is leads. If you give something away and get a listener on your email list, you can follow up, build a relationship, and possibly sell a book or something more valuable later. Don't discount this option for the immediate gratification of selling your book.

What to Do Post-Interview

When your interview is complete, it doesn't mean that you are done with it. Part of leveraging it is helping to give it maximum exposure. Here are three ways to leverage your interview once it's aired.

- As soon as the interview is live, share it on social media and with your email list. This isn't just polite—it shows you're someone worth interviewing. When others see you being featured, it builds your credibility and opens doors to more opportunities.
- Be sure to keep sharing your interviews. Re-sharing doesn't just mean reposting the same link. Share a quote or insight from the interview, or tell a story about how you've applied the advice. Most of your audience won't see every social post or read every email. Reusing interview materials is a way to extend their value for you, your audience, and your former host or interviewer.
- Write articles, blog posts, or newsletters that reference your interview. Share your thoughts on a specific point or highlight a thoughtful question. It's a great way to add value for your audience while continuing to spotlight the interview.

Now that you know the key strategies for obtaining and leveraging interviews, it's time to build your presence. Choose a few shows, prepare your media kit, and confidently pitch. Remember, every interview is an opportunity to grow your audience and strengthen your authority.

TEN

Post-Launch Book Marketing

Jill Celeste, MA

You've released your book—congratulations! It's a beautiful journey, from that first draft to sending your book into the world. Take a moment to celebrate this incredible accomplishment.

But here's where some authors stumble: They assume that once their book is published, the hard work is over—that their book will somehow sell itself over time.

Please don't make that mistake! Your book deserves ongoing, consistent marketing so that it continues reaching the people who need it most. Books don't expire, and neither should your marketing. Whether your book launched last month or five years ago, it still has the potential to impact lives.

Think of book marketing not as a one-time effort but as part of your book's legacy—something that sustains your message, grows your audience, and extends the life of your work.

That's where this chapter comes in.

But before we jump into marketing tactics, we need to focus on something even more important—your mindset. I can teach you every book marketing strategy in the world, but if your mindset isn't in the right place, you won't implement them effectively.

Mindset first, then marketing. Let's dive in.

Shift Your Mindset for Long-Term Book Marketing

As an author and former marketing teacher, I've seen firsthand how mindset myths prevent authors from marketing their books. Let's tackle the five biggest fears that stop authors from embracing ongoing book marketing.

Myth #1: "People are tired of hearing about my book."

I get this one all the time—and I've battled it myself. This fear comes from your Ego, trying to keep you small and safe.

But the truth?

Most people haven't heard about your book yet.

Maybe they didn't open your email, the social media algorithm didn't show them your post, or they were on vacation and unplugged. Whatever the reason, you are not being repetitive. You are allowing new readers to discover your book.

If this fear lingers, try rotating your messaging. Talk about your book from different angles—highlight a reader's testimonial one day, share a behind-the-scenes story another day, then showcase an excerpt the next. This not only improves your marketing but keeps it fresh for you, too!

Myth #2: "It's been too long since my book was published to market it."

Do me a favor: Grab your book and check for an expiration date. I bet you won't find one!

That's because books don't expire. Whether your book was published last week or five years ago, it is still valuable. In fact, many books gain traction years after their release. Here's how to breathe new life into an older book:

- Tie it to a current event or trend. Is there something happening in the world that relates to your book? Use that as a marketing hook.
- Celebrate your book's "birthday." On the anniversary of your book's release, do a special promotion or host a giveaway.
- Create a companion product. Write a workbook, a second edition, or bonus content to reignite interest.

No matter how long ago you published, your book is still worth marketing.

Myth #3: "I don't want to bother people."

Repeat after me: *"I am not bothering anyone by promoting my book."*

Marketing is not about pushing—it's about serving. If your book helps people, why wouldn't you want to tell them about it?

If it helps, shift your language. Instead of saying, "Buy my book," say:

- "If you struggle with X, my book can help."
- "If you love [comparable book], you might enjoy mine, too!"

Your book is a gift—not an intrusion. Own that!

Myth #4: "Other authors are more successful than me."

Hello, Comparison Monster! Yes, some authors may have more sales, bigger platforms, or fancier book deals. But they started from zero just like you did.

When I published *Loud Woman: Goodbye, Inner Good Girl!*, I struggled with impostor syndrome. I kept thinking, "Why would someone read my book when they can read Glennon Doyle's *Untamed* or Denise Duffield-Thomas' *Lucky Bitch*?"

Because *Loud Woman* is *my* story, not Glennon's or Denise's. And my story is worth telling—just like yours is.

Instead of comparing, look to successful authors for inspiration. Study their marketing. What can you adapt for your own book?

Myth #5: "I don't have time for marketing."

Yes, marketing takes time. But if you want to sell books and reach readers, you need to make time for it. Here's how to make book marketing easier and less overwhelming:

- Pick what you enjoy. You don't have to do every marketing tactic—just focus on what excites you.
- Create a marketing habit. Set a specific day of the week for book marketing.
- Use automation tools. Schedule social media posts, emails, and newsletters in advance.

Marketing is like writing—you don't need hours of free time. Small, consistent actions add up.

Joyful and Sustainable Marketing Tactics

Now that we've addressed mindset, let's explore marketing strategies to effectively and easily promote your book.

A word of caution: Marketing your book is like navigating a Las Vegas buffet—so many options, but you don't have to pile everything on your plate. You're not required to implement every tactic I list below. Instead, lean into what brings you joy. When you enjoy your marketing efforts, you'll actually follow through with them—and that consistency is what truly makes a difference. See how that works?

Personal Branding

Your personal brand as an author and expert helps sell books. So you may want to consider how you can market your book through your visibility marketing and personal branding efforts. Add your author title to:

- Social media bios
- Email signatures
- Business cards
- Zoom backgrounds

Use your book as a visual cue:

- Display it on your Zoom calls.
- Carry copies in your car for impromptu sales.
- Use promotional items, such as bookmarks or stickers, to help promote your book (more on this in Chapter 8).
- Use your book cover to create T-shirts, tote bags, and hats (and don't forget to wear them in public!).

Social Media

Most authors rely on social media to market their books, though many have a love-hate relationship with it (and I get it!). The key is to use social media strategically in manageable and effective ways. Here are some tactics to help expand your book's reach.

- Optimize social media profiles by ensuring your book is mentioned in your bio and header graphics.
- Repurpose content to share on your social media profiles. No, no one will notice. You can share excerpts, testimonials, and personal stories.
- Use live video to answer questions from your readers
- Consider a hashtag strategy that could help you reach new audiences through social media.
- Make sure to respond to your readers' comments. Yes, they want to hear from you!

Chapter 5 goes into great depth about social media for authors. Please read the ideas in that chapter because it will help so much!

Content Marketing

Content marketing comes naturally to many writers—you already have the skill! But writing isn't the only way to market your book. Here are some effective content marketing strategies to consider:

- Try blogging and guest writing. You can start your blog or contribute to someone else's.
- Podcasting can significantly enhance your book's reach. You could start your podcast or be a guest on someone else's. Check out Chapter 9 about "Leveraging The Media' to learn more.
- Chapter 3 goes deep into email marketing. Be sure to check out the tips because email marketing is pure gold for author and book promotion!
- Use short-form videos (TikTok, Instagram Reels, YouTube Shorts) to reach new audiences.

Networking

Please don't let networking intimidate you—it doesn't have to be an aggressive, sales-driven experience. Instead, think of it as an opportunity to build genuine relationships.

- Explore in-person opportunities like breakfast meetings or writer's conferences. These events connect you with potential readers, industry pros, and fellow authors.
- Prefer to stay home? Virtual networking lets you connect from your computer—perfect for introverts, time savers, and anyone who'd rather skip the travel.
- Look for chances to speak at networking events. Speaking positions you as an expert and gives you a natural way to promote your book. Some groups welcome guest speakers; others require membership, so ask how to get on the schedule.

- Wherever you network, schedule coffee chats. These thirty-minute conversations—virtual or in person—build deeper connections with no pressure to sell. A book sale may happen, but the real win is the relationship. One conversation can lead to a referral, an opportunity, or even a lifelong friend.

I could go on forever about networking, which is why I delve more into networking in the next chapter.

Turn Engagement Into Action With CTAs

No matter the marketing tactic, a clear call to action (CTA) is essential. A CTA simply tells your audience what to do next—whether it's visiting your website, buying your book, or booking a chat. People want to support you—but they need direction. A clear CTA makes it easy for them to take the next step.

Example Calls to Action

- **Buy my book.** Always include direct purchase links to make it effortless—whether it's your author website, Amazon, or another platform.

- **Download my bonus gift.** Offering free resources like a companion workbook, exclusive chapter, or printable guide is a great way to engage readers while growing your email list.

- **Leave a review.** Make it simple by explaining where to leave the review and why it helps.

- **Share this post.** A perfect CTA for social media and content marketing. You'll be surprised how many people will share your post—just because you asked.

- **Tell a friend.** Word-of-mouth marketing is powerful! Encouraging supporters to recommend your book can lead to new readers, more visibility, and additional sales.

By incorporating strong, intentional calls to action into your marketing, you'll increase engagement, build momentum, and keep your book in the spotlight.

Stay the Course: Habits, Joy, and Community

We've covered a lot in this chapter (honestly, this could be an entire book!), and I hope you're feeling inspired rather than overwhelmed. To keep things simple, here's a to-do list to help you stay on track:

- **Work on your mindset.** Remember, marketing isn't just about selling—it's about sharing your message with the people who need to hear it.

- **Celebrate your wins**. Big or small. Every new reader, every review, and every book sale matters. Acknowledge and appreciate each step forward.

- **Stay consistent.** Marketing requires patience. You probably won't sell 100 books from a single social media post, but consistent action leads to long-term success. Think of it as a marathon, not a sprint—ongoing book marketing follows the same principle.

- **Find a community.** Whether it's a group of three author friends you check in with every week or a larger networking group you meet with monthly, don't do this journey alone. A strong support system makes marketing feel easier and more enjoyable.

- **Choose marketing tactics that bring you joy.**

Here are some ideas to help you find a joyful marketing strategy.

IF YOU LOVE...	TRY THIS STRATEGY
Writing	Blog, guest post, newsletter, book club discussion guides, long social media posts
Talking	Podcasting, virtual author chats, book club appearance, speaking gigs
Designing	Social medai graphics, quote cards, flat lays of your book
Community	Book clubs, local events, reader meetups, networking

And one final thing: *I am rooting for you.* Take imperfect action and trust the process. You—and your story—deserve to be marketed. Never forget that!

ELEVEN

Networking for Authors

Jill Celeste, MA

Does networking make you queasy—like shopping for a used car? I get it. I've seen countless authors cringe at the thought of networking, and honestly, I don't blame them. Too many networking groups still feel like a battlefield of stiff suits, forced smiles, and aggressive business card shuffling. It's all take, take, take—"What can you do for me?"—instead of the real magic of networking: "How can I help you?" It's transactional, and let's be real—it's gross.

But here's the good news: That version of networking is fading. More and more, we're shifting toward something better—networking that feels like collaboration, community, and real relationships.

And here's another truth: Networking isn't just for entrepreneurs and salespeople. It's for authors too.

If you've never considered networking as an author, you might be wondering: How does networking even apply to me? Aren't I just supposed to write great books and let my words do the work?

Not quite.

Authors who network open doors—to marketing opportunities, a growing audience, and the right people to support them on their publishing journey. I know this firsthand. When I published *Loud*

Woman: Good-bye, Inner Good Girl! networking wasn't just helpful—it was essential.

Let me show you exactly how networking made a difference in my book's success.

How Networking Helped Me Launch *Loud Woman*

When I wrote *Loud Woman*, I knew I couldn't just rely on social media posts or hope that people would somehow discover my book. I needed a strategy that would help me reach the right audience, generate buzz, and create lasting momentum.

So, I turned to my network—specifically, my Virtual Networkers community (Virtual Networkers is the weekly virtual networking organization I founded in 2018). Instead of cold marketing tactics, I activated real relationships in natural and effective ways.

Exactly How I Marketed My Book Through Networking

- Held book readings at every Virtual Networkers chapter, giving members a sneak peek of my message.
- Recruited launch partners from the community, providing them with marketing materials so they could easily spread the word on release day.
- I always made sure a copy of *Loud Woman* was visible on my Zoom screen and often wore branded T-shirts to spark conversations.
- Invited Virtual Networkers to write blurbs and reviews, ensuring my book had social proof.
- Built my publishing team from my networking connections, including my editor, publisher, cover designer, and website team.
- Received unwavering support from my community from the first draft to publication day and beyond.

The Result of My Networking Efforts

The result? *Loud Woman* became an Amazon bestseller across multiple categories. It received stellar reviews from respected sources, including Kirkus Reviews, *Midwest Book Review*, and Reedsy.

But the biggest impact wasn't just the sales or rankings—it was the reach. My message spread far and wide because my network believed in it. They didn't just promote my book because I asked them to; they championed it because they trusted me, valued my work, and knew it could help others.

And that's the power of networking.

The best part? You don't have to be a seasoned networker to make this work for you. Whether you're launching your first book or your tenth, networking can provide the support, visibility, and opportunities you need.

So, let's dive into exactly how you can use networking to grow your author career.

How Any Author Can Leverage Networking

Many authors make the mistake of thinking networking is only useful for getting referrals or selling books. But networking is about so much more—it's about connection, community, and building relationships that help you sustain and grow your career.

Finding Readers and Building an Audience

One of the biggest challenges for any author is reaching the right readers. Books don't magically land in the hands of their perfect audience—you have to put yourself where they can find you.

That's where networking comes in. By connecting with people who are genuinely interested in your message, you create relationships that lead to organic book promotion.

These connections can happen in person, through social media, or in virtual networking spaces.

Getting Launch Support

For Book Launch Day, the more people you have rallying behind your book, the bigger your reach. Networking helps you find those supporters who will celebrate your book, amplify your message, and share it with their communities.

Here are some ways you can leverage networking to support your book launch:

- Recruit launch partners who will share your book on their social media and email lists.
- Find book blurbers who will give you advance praise for your book.
- Host pre-launch events like virtual readings or Q&A sessions.
- Tap into influencers such as book bloggers and social media influencers.
- Encourage reviews from your network to boost your book's visibility.

Building an Author Brand

Your brand as an author is more than just your book—it's the story behind why you write and what you stand for. Networking helps establish you as a thought leader in your niche. Here are some ways you can use networking to boost your author brand:

- Public speaking: Get on the speaker calendars at networking groups to share your message.
- Visibility strategies: Wear branded merch, display your

book in the background of virtual meetings, and include book links in your email signature.

- Content collaborations: Connect with bloggers, YouTubers, and podcasters from your networking circles.
- Share content you have created, such as blog posts and YouTube videos, with your network, who may comment or share it for further amplification.

How to Find the Right Networking Group

Okay, I hope you're more on board now! But your next question may be: How do I find the right networking group for me?

Before you start looking for a group, answer these questions in advance. This will help you refine your search.

What Are You Looking for in a Networking Group?

Ask yourself these questions to enable you to be clear on what it is you're looking for in a networking group:

- Do you want to participate in a weekly or monthly networking group? Weekly networking can build deeper connections faster, while monthly meetings may be more manageable if you have a busy schedule.
- Consider your financial investment. Networking groups have varying membership fees, so factor in costs such as annual dues, travel, and meals (if applicable). How much do you want to invest in networking?
- Do you want to network in person or virtually, or both? Be sure to read the next section on why you may want to consider virtual networking.
- Consider the energy of the networking group you want to join—masculine or feminine. Masculine-energy groups are often highly structured, with strict attendance and referral requirements, a rigid meeting agenda, and a strong focus on sales. Feminine-energy groups, on the other hand, emphasize flexibility, collaboration,

relationship-building, and community. Both approaches have value, but knowing what aligns with your networking goals will help you find the right fit.

Once you have these answers, it's time to look for a networking group.

Start Your Search

- Ask fellow authors where they network. Other writers can provide great insights into groups that have worked well for them.
- Do a Google search or look on Meetup and Eventbrite. Many networking groups and writing communities list their meetings online.
- Don't forget that conferences, workshops, and classes count as networking. Attending literary events, book fairs, and writing workshops can be valuable ways to expand your network.

Final Considerations

- Find out how many times you can visit before deciding on membership. Use your guest passes to see if a networking group is a good fit before committing.
- Observe the group's dynamic. Is it collaborative, supportive, and aligned with your values? Some groups are highly structured and transactional, while others focus on relationship-building.
- See if the group has industry alignment. Some groups are general business-focused, while others cater to authors, creatives, or niche communities. Finding one that aligns with your goals can make networking more effective.

Let's talk a little bit more about considering virtual networking and why it might be the best fit for you.

Why Virtual Networking Is Ideal for Authors

Many authors are introverts. Maybe you are, too. If the idea of attending in-person networking events makes you break into a cold sweat, you're not alone. The good news? You don't have to force yourself into a room full of strangers to build a strong author network.

I started Virtual Networkers because I loved networking—but I hated how draining in-person events were. The energy it took to prepare for, attend, and recover from a single lunch meeting meant an entire day lost. As a low-energy introvert, I wanted a better way to connect—one that fit my personality, energy levels, and schedule.

Virtual networking turned out to be the answer. And as an author, it may be a powerful networking method for you because it:

- Saves time and energy
- Expands your reach beyond local connections
- Eliminates social overwhelm
- Fits into your schedule
- Creates a comfortable space to showcase your work

How to Market Your Book Through Networking

Okay, let's get down to some "brass tacks" about how to market your book effectively through networking. By leveraging networking, you can create genuine relationships that lead to organic word-of-mouth promotion and increased visibility. Here are some strategies to market your book in both in-person and virtual networking settings.

In-Person Networking Strategies
When you're networking in person, say at a Business Networking

International (BNI) meeting or writing conference, consider these book promotion tactics:

- Mention your book in your elevator speech/30-second introduction. It could be as simple as "I am NAME, author of TITLE, and ..."
- Bring physical copies of your book. Always have copies available at networking events so you can sell or gift them when appropriate.
- Hand out business cards with your book details. Ensure your card includes your book title, website, and a QR code linking to a purchase page.
- Consider book swag to hand out to your networking peers. This includes bookmarks, bookplates, magnets, or stickers.
- Prop up a copy of your book. If you attend networking events with a table, make sure your book is prominently displayed.
- Offer to do live readings. To generate interest, suggest reading a passage at events, workshops, or book clubs.
- Partner with local businesses. Coffee shops, boutiques, and coworking spaces often support local authors by allowing book signings or stocking copies.

Virtual Networking Strategies

Networking virtually, often through your webcam, also gives you plenty of ways to promote your book. Here are some ideas:

- Make your book visible. Keep a copy of your book behind you during Zoom calls, subtly reinforcing your brand.
- Leverage chat boxes. Share links to your book in networking meetings or virtual events where appropriate.
- Include your book in your introduction. When giving your 30-second intro, mention your book and how it serves your audience.

- Create a virtual background. Design a Zoom background that includes your book cover and website link.
- Host an online book launch. Invite your networking group to attend a virtual book launch or Q&A session about your book.
- Engage in author collaborations. Network with fellow authors for joint book promotions, giveaways, or panel discussions.

What To Say At a Networking Meeting

And if you're feeling a little unsure about what to say at a networking meeting, here are some conversation starters to help you:

- "Hi, I'm [NAME], and I write [GENRE]. I'm here to connect with other creatives and learn how I can support fellow authors."
- "I just finished my first book, and I'm looking for ideas on how to get it in readers' hands. I'd love to hear what's worked for you."
- "What types of books do you like to read?"
- "Who is your favorite author? What do you love about them?"

~

Quick Start Guide: Your First Networking Wins

- Choose one local or virtual networking group to try this month.
- Prepare your thirty-second intro (mention your book!).
- Follow up with one-to-two new connections with a genuine message.
- Add your book link to your email signature.

- Keep your book visible in virtual meetings (background or desk).

Networking surrounds you with the community you need. You don't have to do this alone. Writing may be solitary, but building a successful author career is not. If you're willing to step out of your writing cave and into a community, you'll discover that networking isn't "yucky" or forced—it's an essential part of being a successful, visible, and well-supported author.

Your readers are waiting—your message matters. And the right network can help you reach the people who need your book the most.

TWELVE

Leveraging Events and Tours

Deborah Kevin, MA

Publishing your book is a huge milestone—but the work doesn't stop when you hit "publish." In fact, that's when the magic of reader engagement begins.

Book clubs, indie bookstores, and libraries are powerful, often underutilized allies in your ongoing author visibility strategy. These communities don't just provide visibility—they offer connection, conversation, and the kind of word-of-mouth momentum that algorithms can only dream about.

Let's explore how to approach these venues, build meaningful relationships, and prepare yourself for book events that don't just sell books—but create superfans.

Book Clubs: Small Groups, Big Impact

Book clubs are the unsung heroes of post-launch book life. Whether they meet in living rooms, libraries, or online, book clubs are intimate spaces where your story is truly *discussed*—not just skimmed. These groups can fuel word-of-mouth buzz, offer invaluable feedback, and create genuine relationships between authors and readers.

Where to Find Book Clubs:

- Ask friends and colleagues if they belong to any (or know someone who does).
- Reach out to your local library or bookstore to see if they host groups.
- Explore online platforms like Facebook, Meetup, Goodreads, or Bookclubs.com.
- Consider genre-specific clubs or those centered on themes relevant to your book.

Pro Tip: Offer to Zoom into a club's meeting as a guest. Book clubs love author drop-ins—especially when paired with fun Q&As or signed bookplates as gifts.

Independent Bookstores: Community Champions

Independent bookstores are the heartbeat of many local communities—and they love to support authors, especially local or indie ones. These stores offer more than shelf space; they host readings, signings, launch parties, and cozy in-store conversations.

How to Connect With Indie Bookstores:

- Use sites like Bookshop.org, IndieBound, and the American Booksellers Association to locate stores in your area or genre niche.
- Follow them on social media and comment on their posts to build awareness before reaching out.
- Attend their events and say hello. A little IRL love goes a long way.

Pro Tip: Team up with another local author and pitch a joint event. Bookstores love collaborative events—they double the audience and cross-promotional power.

Sample Outreach Email to Bookstores:

Dear [Bookstore Manager's Name],

As a local author and longtime fan of [Bookstore Name], I wanted to introduce myself and share the exciting news that my book, *[Title]*, launches on [Date]. It's available in both print and digital formats and I'd love to explore opportunities to collaborate—whether that's stocking the book, scheduling an author event, or just starting a conversation.

I've attached my media kit, which includes all the book details and contact information.

I'd love to connect and look forward to hearing from you!

Warmly,
[Your Name]

Libraries: A Long Game Worth Playing

Libraries are community powerhouses that elevate local authors, support lifelong readers, and—let's not forget—actually purchase books for their shelves. Plus, they often host author talks, signings, and panel discussions.

Don't overlook your local branch or even your hometown library. Librarians are book lovers at heart—and often enthusiastic advocates for local talent.

Ways to Engage With Libraries:

- Offer to do a free author talk or Q&A (virtual or in-person).
- Donate a copy or ask to be added to their acquisitions list.
- Reach out to your hometown, high school, or college libraries with a personal connection.
- Use WorldCat.org to find US libraries in your area.

Sample Outreach Email to Libraries:

Dear [Librarian's First Name],

As a proud supporter of [Library Name] and a newly published local author, I'd love to introduce my book, *[Title]*, which launches on [Date]. It's available in both print and digital formats (including a cost-per-checkout option).

I've attached my media guide with all the details, and I'd be honored if you'd consider featuring it in your collection or inviting me to speak with your patrons.

Please feel free to reach out if you have any questions!

Warm regards,
[Your Name]

Why Book Events Matter

Book events—whether held in indie stores, living rooms, Zoom rooms, or library halls—give authors something that no paid ad ever can: real, human connection. They create memorable reader experiences. They make your book personal. And they build buzz in the best way possible: through conversations, not just clicks.

Beyond visibility, book events offer:

- Personal Connection: Readers become fans when they meet you face-to-face.
- Media Moments: Events can attract local coverage or online buzz.
- Sales Spike: Signed books or in-the-moment purchases are powerful (and often emotional!) buying triggers.

Planning Your Own Book Tour—Live or Virtual

Ready to step into the spotlight? Consider these event-building strategies:

- **Partner With Indie Bookstores:** They have the space, the audience, and the promotional muscle.
- **Use Virtual Platforms:** Zoom, Crowdcast, and Instagram Live allow for intimate, accessible readings and Q&As.
- **Engage Book Clubs Directly:** Offer to lead discussions or attend their meetings.
- **Cross-Promote With Other Authors:** Double your impact by sharing audiences.

Pro Tip: Use the power of "and." Do local *and* virtual. In-person *and* hybrid. Small group *and* big event. Flexibility creates reach.

Final Thoughts

Book events aren't just nice-to-haves—they're core to your post-launch visibility strategy. Whether you're signing stock in a cozy indie store, laughing over wine with a book club, or Zooming into a library in another state, these are the moments that make your book *real* for readers.

Say yes. Show up. Stay connected. Your next reader is waiting to meet you.

Resource and Links

Author Brand Illustrations: https://broterandbeatty.com/illustrations-for-authors-tool-kit/

Nonfiction book website example: https://broterandbeatty.com/non-fiction-book-page/

Fiction book website example: https://broterandbeatty.com/fiction-book/

To access all of the aforementioned illustrations and examples, you can use this handy-dandy QR code:

Endnotes

[1] *Naruto v. Slater*, 888 F.3d 418 (9th Cir. 2018).

[2] *Feist Publications, Inc. v. Rural Tel. Serv. Co.*, 499 U.S. 340 (1991)

[3] *Fourth Estate Public Corp v. Wall-Street. com, LLC,* 139 S. Ct. 81, 586 US __, 203 L. Ed. 2d 147 (Supreme Court, 2019)

[4] Wells, Tom. "13 Crucial Amazon Book Sales Statistics in 2025 (U.S. & World)." Marketing Scoop, November 26, 2023. https://www.marketingscoop.com/small-business/amazon-book-sales-statistics/.

[5] Saxena, Esha. "27 Important Book Sales Statistics to Know (2024 Data)." GrabOn Blog - Powered by GrabOn.com, May 12, 2025. https://grabon.com/blog/book-sales-statistics/.

About the Authors

Cheri D. Andrews, Esquire, is an award-winning small business attorney. Cheri has helped hundreds of heart-centered small business owners get legally compliant and protected, providing them confidence and peace of mind. Cheri is the best-selling author of *Smooth Sailing: An Essential Guide to Legally Protecting Your Business*, a sought-after speaker, and the founder of The Wise Owl Academy. She enjoys digital scrapbooking, mixed media art, reading, and travel, but her greatest joy is hanging with her family. Learn more at cheriandrews.com.

Sandra Beatty has been a conversion copywriter since 2017. She studied under two of Amy Porterfield's copywriters, has written for several prolific and best-selling authors, and is a published author herself. Her predominant area of expertise is website conversion copy and strategy. She has a passion for teaching, and you'll often find her on YouTube or partnering up with her favorite graphic designer, Hanne Brøter, showing business owners how to boost their website conversions. Learn more at sandrabeatty.com.

Hanne Brøter is a graphic designer, visual branding expert, and teacher of graphic design. Her passion is helping entrepreneurs create and maintain a visual look of their businesses that reflects their brand message in a unique and authentic way. She works with entrepreneurs through her business, Your Brand Vision, and through the Brøter School of Design, where she teaches graphic design to non-designers who want to leverage the power of correct graphic design in their marketing. Learn more at YourBrandVision.com.

Jill Celeste, MA, is a low-energy introvert on a high-energy mission to change how women network. She founded Virtual Networkers to build connection and sisterhood—minus the "ick" of traditional networking. Author of *Loud Woman: Goodbye, Inner Good Girl!* (and more), Jill lives in South Carolina with her family and four scene-stealing pets—Mr. Wu, Calamity Jane, Trixie, and Ellsworth—all named after characters from HBO's *Deadwood*. Learn more at virtualnetworkers.biz.

Deborah Kevin is the founder of Highlander Press, host of the STORYTELLHER podcast, and an unapologetic disruptor of the status quo. A proud alum of Stanford University's Creative Writing Program (novel emphasis) and holder of a master's degree in publishing from Western Colorado University, Debby brings both deep expertise and heart to every project she touches. She's the author of *Shelf Life* and several nonfiction works, with her next novel currently in development. A magic believer, French Press coffee enthusiast, and master of irreverent humor, she's passionate about elevating women's voices, challenging the status quo, and helping changemakers tell the stories that shape our world. Learn more at deborahkevin.com.

Jennifer Nichols is a social media confidence coach, author, and speaker who helps business owners take the WTF out of social media. With a passion for empowering women, she helps clients overcome fear, find their voice, and create authentic, effective content. Through her writing and coaching, Jennifer turns stress into strategy, making social media approachable. Her mission is to help others break free from doubt and show up confidently to connect with their ideal audience. Visit bloomandhustle.com to learn more.

Suzanne Tregenza helps non-fiction authors focus on revenue and thought leadership status. Since leaving her six-figure job, Suzanne has employed her MBA in marketing and entrepreneurship, along with personal experience from living in the weeds of her business, to support clients with strategy, marketing, technology, delegation, and mindset. Clients describe her as "invaluable" and a "gentle butt-kicker." She is the best-selling author of *Hang on Tight! Learn to Love the Roller Coaster of Entrepreneurship*. Learn more at suzannetmoore.com.

Copyright Details

About the Publisher

Founded in 2019, Highlander Press is a vibrant, mid-sized publishing house dedicated to transforming the world through the power of words. We are deeply committed to diversity and bringing big ideas to the forefront. At Highlander Press, we help authors navigate the journey from initial concept through writing, editing, and publishing, culminating in the release of a book that not only fulfills a lifelong dream but also solidifies their expertise and boosts their confidence.

Our unique approach centers on forging strong, collaborative relationships with women-owned businesses across the publishing spectrum, including graphic design, marketing, launching, copyright management, and publicity. We believe in the power of community and operate by the mantra, "a rising tide lifts all boats." This philosophy not only enhances our business model but also ensures that our authors receive unparalleled support and opportunities to succeed.

Join us in making a mark in the literary world, where your voice is heard, and your message has the power to change lives.

facebook.com/highlanderpress

instagram.com/highlanderpress

tiktok.com/highlanderpress

linkedin.com/company/highlander-press

Also From Highlander Press

Anthologies

Becoming Unstoppable

Heart-Centered Marketing: Proven Strategies that Naturally Attract and Nurture Clients

Your First Year: What I Wish I'd Known

Bestselling Books

Line Magic by Kris Faatz

Shelf Life: A Field Guide to Long Term Author Success by Deborah Kevin, MA

Sometimes I Think I Suck by Tal Fagin

In Motion by Joanne Flynn Black

Burnt Gloveboxes (Vol. II) by Gina Ramsey

Free Spirit at Free Safety by Joe Zagorski

Gray Matter by Avery Volz

Fourteen Stones by Kris Faatz

Smooth Sailing (2nd Ed.) by Cheri Andrews, Esq.

Juris Ex Machina by John W. Maly

The Knowing by Kimberly Patton

Thriving Through Cancer by Kelly Lutman

Burnt Gloveboxes (Vol. I) by Gina Ramsey

The Selfish Hour by Megan Weisheipl

Intuitive Languages by Nicole Meltzer

What Color Am I? by Sarah Patterson

Smooth Sailing by Cheri Andrews, Esq.

Peace in Passing (2nd Ed.) by Maribeth Decker

Hang on Tight! by Suzanne Tregenza Moore

A Path of Oneness by Ellen Feldman

Loud Woman by Jill Celeste, MA

By a Thread by Nicolette Blanco

Your 4 Truths by Judy Kane

You, Me, and Anxiety series by Dr. Robyn Reu Graham

That First Client (2nd Ed.) by Jill Celeste

You've Written Your Book. Now What? by Deborah Kevin

The Gift of Loss by Cathy Agasar

30 Second Success by Laura Templeton

Children's Titles

Betty Bartholomew and the Vanishing Begonias by Connie Jo Miller

Sara Smitherson and the Disappearing Snickerdoodles by Connie Jo Miller

Penelope Parsons and the Missing Pomegranates by Connie Jo Miller

My Body Knows. Do I Know? by Ashley Cournoyer-Smith

Meatball and Birdie by Elle Fox

Glitter Bird by Angie Bird

Lauren and Val Take a Walk by Lauren Eileen

Forthcoming Titles

StoryShift by Anne Fowler Wade

Ripples on the Church Water by Brynn MacDonald

Animal Mayhem (Burnt Gloveboxes III) by Gina Ramsey

Finding Grace by Deborah Kevin

www.ingramcontent.com/pod-product-compliance
Lightning Source LLC
Chambersburg PA
CBHW052020030426

42335CB00026B/3221